> Dedicated to John Baptist Kotmair, Jr.
> who has taught many the principles of
> our **Great Constitution**
> the Supreme Law of the Land.

"Woe unto them that decree unrighteous decrees, and that write grievousness *which* they have prescribed; To turn aside the needy from judgment, and to take away the right from the poor of my people, that widows may be their prey, and *that* they may rob the fatherless! And what will ye do in the day of visitation, and in the desolation *which* shall come from far? To whom will ye flee for help? And where will you leave your glory? Without me they shall bow down under the prisoners, and they shall fall under the slain. For all this his anger is not turned away, but his hand *is* stretched out still."

-ISAIAH 10 : 1- 4

"Let the high praises of God be in their mouth, and a two-edged sword in their hand; To execute vengeance upon the heathen, and punishments upon the people; To bind their kings with chains and their nobles with fetters of iron; To execute upon them the judgment written; This honour have all his saints. Praise ye the LORD."

-PSALM 149 : 6 - 9

"IT IS ERROR ALONE THAT NEEDS THE SUPPORT OF GOVERNMENT, TRUTH CAN STAND BY ITSELF."

-THOMAS JEFFERSON

HOW TO USE THIS BOOK

1. Make a decision to become a *voracious* reader. Definition: "VORA'CIOUS, a. [adjective] 1. Greedy for eating; ravenous; very hungry... 2. Rapacious; eager to devour;... 3. Ready to swallow up..." (Noah Webster -1828) The preservation of our Republic depends upon the right and righteous actions of a fully informed citizenry!

2. Familiarize yourself with all the sections of this book so you can turn back and forth from the notes and helps to the text of the 1828 Catechism. (The Table of Contents is on page 1)

3. Obtain a copy of Noah Webster's 1828 Dictionary. Only the 1828 edition will do! This is the monumental work of Noah Webster the "Founding Father" of American Education. (You may write us for ordering information)

4. Read the Constitution and the Bible (The Founders and Framers regarded the Bible as the best book on government). There is absolutely no substitute for reading all these materials until your comprehension is complete. The rewards for all of this labor are immeasurable but ironically you will never own them unless you make the effort. Liberty is not *free*! The price we must pay is "eternal vigilance" and tireless effort. Right knowledge is the first step toward proper action!

5. Whenever you have *any* doubt as to the proper meaning of a word, do not continue reading until you understand what it means in context. Consult the 1828 Webster's and read all the definitions and notes on that word. If Webster's definition includes a Scripture reference, look it up in a King James Version of the Holy Bible. Even if you *think* you know the meaning of a word you will often find that the 1828 Webster's definition will help clarify a particular aspect. The same procedure applies to concepts and principles.

6. Read the Declaration of Independence and the Constitution until you can articulate all their concepts and defend all of their principles. Remember as you read, you are searching out your birthright as a Sovereign Citizen of the Greatest Nation on Earth! You are ultimately the one on whom the enforcement of a "Government of Law and Not of Men" depends!

7. Read all of the other available documents mentioned anywhere in this book, particularly in the list on page 53. Never settle for just reading *about* the Great American Statesmen. This is an intellectual trap and one of the most obvious flaws in *politically correct* "history" (i.e. The cherry tree myth about George Washington is a poor substitute for his *Farewell Address*). You must read the Founders' and Framers' *words* until you comprehend their thoughts well enough to approach contemporary problems and know without a doubt, that you are applying the same principles in the same ways that they would if they were alive today.

8 Ask fellow citizens the questions in this Catechism and have fellow citizens read them to you. Share these timeless truths wherever you go! Teach them to your children, your grandchildren, your parents and your grandparents. Study them until your answers are reflexive. This is a better heritage for your children than all the material wealth in the world! Make sure everyone you know has access to and can understand this book and all of these principles. It is your great privilege as an American to have access to the documents containing the most sublime thought on self government that ever moved pen to paper! If you will work diligently at it, you can learn to think the thoughts of these great Statesmen after them. Only then will you begin to appreciate their legacy.

Remember, "...this precious Constitution, thus wise, thus just, is your birth-right. It has been earned for you by your fathers, who counselled much, labored long, and shed their dearest blood, to win it for their children. To them, it was the fruit of toil and danger --- to you, it is a gift. Do not slight it on that account, but prize it as you ought. It is yours, no human power can deprive you of it but your own folly and wickedness. To undervalue, is one of the surest ways to lose it. Take pains to know what the Constitution is ---the more you study, the higher you will esteem it. The better you understand your own rights, the more likely you will be to preserve and guard them."

-- Arthur J. Stansbury

**May God grant that you too, will pledge
your life, your fortune and your sacred Honour!**

Remember, "**To be free, you must live free!**" - John Baptist Kotmair, Jr.

• **To Attend or Arrange a Seminar in Your Area** •

Write:

William H. Huff

**12 Carroll Street #119
Westminster, MD 21157**

Phone:

(410) 374-4255

"RESISTANCE TO TYRANNY IS SERVICE TO GOD." !!! - JEFFERSON

"Our country is in danger, but not to be despaired of...On you depend the fortunes of America. You are to decide the important question, on which rest the happiness and liberty of millions yet unborn. Act worthy of yourselves."

-Dr. Joseph Warren
(Speaking at Boston on March 5, 1775 on the anniversary of the "Boston Massacre")

"*Honour, justice* and *humanity* call upon us to hold, and to transmit to our posterity, that liberty, which we received from our ancestors. It is not our duty to leave wealth to our children: but it is our duty, to leave liberty to them. No infamy, iniquity, or cruelty can exceed our own, if we, born and educated in a country of freedom, intitled to its blessings, and knowing their value, pusillanimously deserting the post assigned to us by Divine Providence, surrender succeeding generations to a condition of wretchedness, from which no human efforts, in all probability, will be sufficient to extricate them; the experience of all states mournfully demonstrating to us, that when arbitrary power has been established over them, even the wisest and bravest nations, that ever flourished, have, in a few years, degenerated into abject and wretched vassals."

(from the *Resolutions of Committee for the Province of Pennsylvania* - 1774)

"...the preservation of the sacred fire of liberty, and the destiny of the Republican model of Government, are justly considered as deeply, perhaps as finally staked, on the experiment entrusted to the hands of the American people."

-George Washington

"But we want no excuse for the *supposed* mistakes of our ancestors. Let us first see it proved that they were mistakes. 'Till then we must hold ourselves obliged to them for the sentiments transmitted to us so worthy of their character, and so important to our security:... "

-Samuel Adams

Read the words of the United States supreme Court in:

South Carolina v. United States, **199 U.S. 437 (1905) at pages 448-449:**

"The Constitution is a written instrument. As such its meaning does not alter. That which it meant when adopted it means now. Being a grant of powers to a government its language is general, and as changes come in social and political life it embraces in its grasp all new conditions which are within the scope of the powers in terms conferred. In other words, while the powers granted do not change, they apply from generation to generation to all things to which they are in their nature applicable. This in no manner abridges the fact of its changeless nature and meaning. **Those things which are within its grants of power, as those grants were understood when made, are still within them, and those things not within them remain still excluded.** As said by Mr. Chief Justice Taney in *Dred Scott v. Sandford,* 10 How. 393, 426:

> " ' It is not only the same in words, but the same in meaning, and delegates the same powers to the Government, and reserves and secures the same rights and privileges to the citizens; and *as long as it continues to exist in its present form*, it speaks not only in the same words, **but with the same meaning and intent with which it spoke when it came from the hands of its framers, and was voted on and adopted by the people of the United States. Any other rule of construction would abrogate the judicial character of this court, and make it the mere reflex of popular opinion or passion of the day.** '

"It must be remembered that the framers of the Constitution were not mere visionaries, toying with speculations or theories, but practical men, dealing with the facts of political life as they understood them, putting into form the government they were creating, and prescribing in language clear and intelligible the powers that government was to take. Mr. Chief Justice Marshall, in *Gibbons v. Ogden,* 9 Wheat. 1, 188, well declared:

> " ' **As men whose intentions require no concealment, generally employ the words which most directly and aptly express the ideas they intend to convey, the enlightened patriots who framed our Constitution, and the people who adopted it, must be understood to have employed words in their natural sense, and to have intended what they have said.** ' "

(Emphasis Added)

ELEMENTARY CATECHISM

on the

CONSTITUTION

of the

UNITED STATES

FOR THE USE OF THE SCHOOLS

ARTHUR J. STANSBURY -1828

EDITED by WILLIAM H. HUFF -1993

Surpassing Wisdom from the Father of our Country

"...It is important, likewise, that the habits of thinking in a free Country should inspire caution in those entrusted with its administration, to confine themselves within their respective Constitutional spheres; avoiding the exercise of Powers of one department to encroach upon another. The spirit of encroachment tends to consolidate the powers of all the departments in one, and thus to create whatever the form of government, a real despotism. A just estimate of that love of power, and proneness to abuse it, which predominates in the human heart is sufficient to satisfy us of the truth of this position. The necessity of reciprocal checks in the exercise of political power; by dividing and distributing it into different depositories, and constituting each the Guardian of the Public Weal against invasions by the others, has been evinced by experiments ancient and modern; some of them in our own country and under our own eyes. To preserve them must be as necessary as to institute them. If in the opinion of the People, the distribution or modification of the Constitutional powers be in any particular wrong, let it be corrected by an amendment in the way which the Constitution designates. But let there be no change by usurpation; for though this, in one instance, may be the instrument of good, it is the customary weapon by which free governments are destroyed. The precedent must always greatly overbalance in permanent evil any partial or transient benefit which the use can at any time yield.

    Of all the dispositions and habits which lead to political prosperity, Religion and morality are indispensable supports. In vain would that man claim the tribute of Patriotism, who should labor to subvert these great Pillars of human happiness, these firmest props of the duties of Men and citizens. The mere Politician, equally with the pious man ought to respect and cherish them. A volume could not trace their connections with private and public felicity. Let it simply be asked where is the security for property, for reputation, for life, if the sense of religious obligation desert our oaths, which are the instruments of investigation in Courts of Justice? And let us indulge with caution the supposition, that morality can be maintained without religion. Whatever can be conceded to the influence of refined education on minds of peculiar structure, reason and experience both forbid us to expect that National morality can prevail in exclusion of religious principle..."

- George Washington in his Farewell Address on the 17th of September, 1796.

© Copyright 1993 at Common Law by William H. Huff - All Rights Reserved
•Revised October 23, 1995•

## Table of Contents	Page

Quotations and supreme Court case law	I-II
Table of Contents	1
Preface to this Edition	2
Stansbury's 1828 Preface	3
Stansbury's 1828 Catechism	**4-46**
Stansbury's Conclusion	47
Editor's Notes	48-52
Appendix	53-95
The Declaration of Independence	**58-62**
Paper Money Discussion and Vote	63,64
Franklin Recommends the New Constitution	65-67
Franklin's "Prophecy"	68
The United States Constitution	**69-92**
The Virginia Resolutions of 1798 and 1799	93,94
Article: "No Strings Attached?"	95

FOR ADDITIONAL INFORMATION,
MATERIALS, VIDEOS, SEMINARS,
WRITE or CALL:

William H. Huff
12 Carroll Street #119
Westminster, MD 21157

Phone: (410) 374-4255

PREFACE

The following is a Catechism was written during the time between the Framing of the United States Constitution and the death of James Madison who has been called the Father of the Constitution. In order to promote a candid and thorough discussion of all issues related to correcting flaws in the Articles of Confederation (the document that had previously bound the States into what many considered an inadequate and weak union) Madison had pledged not to reveal the contents of his notes on the convention during the lifetimes of any who had attended. This pledge he scrupulously kept until his death in 1835. During the administration of President Andrew Jackson (all of the other Framers having previously died) Madison's widow Dolly sold the notes to the Congress as her late husband had instructed.

Since Arthur J. Stansbury could not have had access to the original notes of the Convention, some notable errors were made. This is not to cast aspersions on the author or to deprecate his work, but mainly to point out how great care and thorough research need to attend any effort to understand the Constitution as conceived by the Framers *in its original intent*. These great men were framing *the supreme Law of the Land!*

Following the notes at the end of this edition, I have inserted excerpts from *The Formation of the Union of the United States,* which is a publication commissioned by Act of Congress in 1926. This collection of the great documents is now quite rare and we should all encourage our Senators and Representatives in Washington to propose a resolution ordering the printing and distribution of many more copies. Its pages contain the solutions to many, if not all of our present woes as a nation.

I have not undertaken to correct every flaw or extol every virtue of the original 1828 Catechism, but I believe this edition provides a good place to start for generations alive today that are beginning to discover the many truths that have either been deliberately hidden or enshrouded in ignorance and neglect.

The current "progress" toward global totalitarian socialism stands in stark contrast to the founding principles that forged this great nation. If there is not a revival of spiritual as well as political understanding in this generation, we may be the last to have even a rudimentary understanding of the great liberty that was to be secured by these sacred documents that form the foundations of this great Republic!

To the Framers of the United States Constitution, liberty and responsibility were inseparable. May God grant that we realize the same!

- William H. Huff

PREFACE to Original 1828 Stansbury Edition

That a people living under a free government which they have themselves originated should be well acquainted with the instrument which contains it, needs not to be proved. Were the system, indeed, very cumbrous and extensive, running into minute detail, and hard to be retained in the memory, even this would be no good reason why pains should not be taken to understand and imprint it upon the mind but when its principles are simple, its features plain and obvious, and its brevity surpassing all example, it is certainly a most reprehensible negligence to remain in ignorance of it. ---Yet how small a portion of the citizens of this Republic have even a tolerable acquaintance with their own Constitution? It has appeared to the author of the following sheets that this culpable want of acquaintance with what is of such deep interest to us all, is to be traced to the omission of an important part of what ought to be an American education, viz. the study of the civil institutions of our country. ---We prize them, it is true, and are quite enough in the habit of boasting about them: would it not be well to teach their elements to those whose best inheritance they are?

The following work has been prepared with a view to such an experiment. It is written expressly for the use of boys, and it has been the aim and effort of the writer to bring down the subject completely to a level with their capacity to understand it. Whether he has succeeded the trial must show. He has purposely avoided all abstruse questions, and has confined himself to a simple, common-sense explanation of each article. It is very possible some inaccuracies may be discovered; and should this be the case, they shall be carefully corrected, should the work be so far approved as to reach another edition.

In the mean time he cannot but indulge the hope, that in laying this little offering upon the altar of our country, he has rendered her an acceptable service.

-A. J. S.

ELEMENTARY CATECHISM

Question 1. In what country do you live?
Answer. In the United States of America.

Q2. Why is this country called the United States?
A. Because it is made up of a number of States which were once separate, but afterwards agreed to *unite* together.

Q3. What do you mean by a state?
A. I mean any district of country whose people are all under one government.

Q4. Had then the different States which united together, each a government of its own?
A. Yes; but they agreed to put themselves all under one general government.

Q5. Why did they do this?
A. Because it would promote their general welfare.

Q6. Is some government necessary in every country?
A. Certainly; without it nobody would be safe: not only our property, but our lives would be in danger.

Q7. Cannot all the people of a country govern themselves?
A. If every man was perfectly virtuous, and knew what would be best for himself and others, they might. But this is far from being the case; and therefore the people of every country are and must be governed.

Q8. How is this done?
A. Laws are made which all must obey; whoever disobeys them is punished.

Q9. Who makes these laws?
A. They are made in different ways, under different governments. In some countries a *single man* makes the laws according to his own pleasure.

Q10. What is such a government called?
A. A *Despotism*, or absolute monarchy: and the person who thus rules is a Despot, or absolute monarch. In other states a certain number of persons belonging to ancient or wealthy families make the laws.

Q11. What is such a government styled?

A. An *Aristocracy* or oligarchy.
In other cases the people themselves meet to make the laws. This is called a pure *Democracy*.

Q12. A state must be very small where all the people can meet in one assembly.
A. This form of government is only suited to a small city, or rather village, and can never take place in a state of any extent. One other form remains; this is, where the people, too numerous to meet, themselves, choose certain of their own number to meet for them. This is called a **REPRESENTATIVE GOVERNMENT**, because those who meet *represent* all the rest. It is also called a **REPUBLIC**.

Q13. Which of these ways of governing a nation is the best?
A. The last. A country thus ruled is said to be *free*, or to enjoy *liberty*: but where a single man may make what laws he pleases, and all the rest must obey him, the people are no better than slaves.

Q14. Why do they obey him?
A. Because he has an army of soldiers whom he pays, and who force the people to obedience.

Q15. Cannot they raise an army too, and resist him?
A. This has sometimes been done, and after much bloodshed and confusion, the people have partially succeeded; but they have more frequently failed, and then they were more oppressed than before.

Q16. How is this country governed?
A. It is a Republic, and is governed by persons whom the people choose from time to time to make the laws.

Q17. Was it always a Republic?
A. No. The states were formerly *Colonies*.

Q18. What do you mean by Colonies?
A. When a part of the people of a nation remove to some distant place, where they settle, but still continue to be governed by the nation from which they came out, these new settlements are called Colonies, and the country which governs them is called the *mother country*.

Q19. By what nation were the American Colonies governed?
A. By Great Britain. Most of the people who first settled this country came from England, Scotland or Ireland, (which three countries make up Great Britain) and long after they had settled here, continued to be governed by laws most of which were made in England.

Q20. Were these laws good and wise?
A. Many of them were; and for a time the colonies were perhaps better off than if they had entirely governed themselves, because, though Great Britain did rule them, she also gave them protection by her fleets, and did many things for their advantage. But afterward very unwise and unjust laws were made, and such as threatened to destroy all liberty in the colonies.

Q21. What did the colonies do then?
A. They made complaints, and reasoned for a long time with Great Britain, trying to persuade her to act more justly.

Q22. Did Great Britain listen to their complaints and repeal those bad laws?
A. No--but instead of that sent over ships and soldiers to force us to obey them.

Q23. And did we obey?
A. No; the people of the colonies consulted with each other what was to be done, and at length took up arms, raised such armies as they could, and though they had few soldiers, no experienced officers, and but little money, they carried on a war against the whole power of Great Britain, and having (with aid from France) forced two British armies to lay down their arms and surrender themselves prisoners, they at length compelled Great Britain to acknowledge their independence.

Q24. What do you mean by that?
A. I mean that she was compelled to consent that all those colonies, which had before been governed by laws made for them by her, should after that have liberty to make laws for themselves, and obey her no more.

Q25. When we speak of this war, what do we call it?
A. We call it the American Revolution.

Q26. What do you mean by Revolution?
A. A revolution means some great change of government; and we ought ever to remember ours with ardent gratitude to God for so great a blessing, and with lasting love and reverence for those good, wise, and brave men, who went through such dangers and sufferings that their country might be free.

Q27. When and where did the war of the revolution begin?
A. At Lexington and Concord, villages near Boston in Massachusetts, on the 19th of April, 1775.

Q28. How long did the struggle continue?
A. More than seven years.

Q29. When did it end?

A. On the 21st of January, 1783, when a treaty was signed at Paris acknowledging the independence of the United States.

Q30. Why is the 4th of July kept with such public rejoicing through all parts of the United States?
A. Because on the 4th of July, 1776 the Colonies first declared themselves free and independent; from that day the independence of the country is reckoned in all our public proceeding; though it was not acknowledged by Great Britain till 1783.

Q31. What was the change produced by the Revolution?
A. The different Colonies became each a free STATE, having power to govern itself in any way it should think proper.

Q32. Had not one state any power over the other?
A. None at all - and the several states might have remained entirely distinct countries, as much as France and Spain.

Q33. Did they?
A. No. Having been led to unite together to help each other in the war, they soon began to find that it would be much better for each of them that they should all continue in its farther prosecution, and accordingly they entered into an agreement (which was called a *Confederation*) in which they made some laws which they all agreed to obey; but after their independence was obtained, finding the defects of this plan, they called a Convention in which they laid a complete plan for uniting all the states under one GENERAL GOVERNMENT - this plan is called THE FEDERAL CONSTITUTION. On this great plan, or Constitution the safety and happiness of the United States does, under Almighty God, mainly depend: all our laws are made by its direction or authority; whoever goes contrary to it injures and betrays his country, injures you, injures me, betrays us all, and is deserving of the heaviest punishment. Whoever, on the contrary, loves and keeps it sacred, is his country's friend, secures his own safety, and farthers the happiness of all around him. Let every American learn, from his earliest years, to love, cherish and obey the Constitution. Without this he can neither be a great or a good citizen; without this his name will never be engraved with honor in the pages of our history, nor transmitted, like that of Washington, with praises and blessings to a late posterity.

Q34. You say that in a republic the laws are made by certain persons whom the people choose for that purpose: who make the laws in our republic?
A. The laws which concern only one of the states are made by persons chosen by the people of that state, and who, when met, are called the *Legislature*, the *General Assembly;* or the *General Court* of that particular state. Those, for instance, who make laws which concern only the state of New York, are called the Legislature of the state of New York; those who make laws which concern only the state of Massachusetts, are called the General Court of Massachusetts.

But laws which concern all the states or more states than one are made by the CONGRESS OF THE UNITED STATES.

Q35. But if even the Congress itself should make a law which is contrary to the *Constitution,* must the people obey it?
A. No.

Q36. Who is to determine whether any law is contrary to the Constitution or no, the people themselves?
A. No: but certain persons whom they have appointed, [called Judges of the Supreme Court of the United States.] *

Q37. Do the members of the Congress of the United States all meet together in one assembly, when they make the laws?
A. No: they meet in two separate assemblies, one of which is called the SENATE, and the other is called the HOUSE OF REPRESENTATIVES.

Q38. Who choose the persons who shall be members of the House of Representatives?
A. The people of all the different states: because the laws of Congress concern all the states, and must be obeyed by all the people of this Republic.

Q39. Have boys a right to choose them?
A. No: boys are too young.

Q40. Are any other persons unfit?
A. Yes.

Q41. How is it determined who may, and who may not choose them?
A. By the laws of each state. - Whoever is allowed to choose the members of the Legislature of any state, is also allowed by the Constitution to choose members of the House of Representatives of the United States. - Some states allow one class of persons to choose and other states allow a different class - each state acts as it thinks best. This choice is called an Election.

Q42. How is it conducted?
A. On a day fixed before hand, and publicly known, the people who are to choose, and who are called *voters*, meet at certain places called the *Polls*: here persons sit called *Inspectors*, who have certain boxes called *ballot boxes* before them, and each person who votes puts into the hole in the top of these boxes a piece of paper with the names of the persons whom he chooses written or printed on it. These pieces of paper are afterwards examined and counted by the Inspectors, who keep a written account of the names voted for, and the number of votes given by the people for each. The persons having the greatest number of votes

---

* See Editor's Notes on Pages 48-52 after the Catechism. It is critical that you read all of the notes. You are encouraged to write us with your criticisms and comments and help us to improve this work in a later edition.

are chosen. There are some slight differences in the mode of holding elections in the different states, but it is the same in every important particular.

Q43. Are the times, places, and manner of holding these elections fixed by Congress?
A No. They have, thus far, been left to be regulated by each state for itself, but Congress may fix them if it thinks fit.

Q44. Suppose a dispute should arise concerning an election, and one person shall declare that he has been fairly chosen, while another denies it, and insists that he himself has been chosen; who has the power to settle the dispute?
A. A dispute between persons who claim a seat in the House of Representatives can be determined only by the House of Representatives; a dispute between persons claiming a seat in the Senate can be settled by the Senate only. Such disputes frequently arise.

Q45. When a person is chosen to be a Member of the House of Representatives, how long does he continue so?
A. For two years.

Q46. When the two years have expired, may he be chosen again?
A. Yes.

Q47. Suppose he dies before the time is out?
A. Another is chosen in his stead, for the rest of the time.

Q48. How old must a person be before he can be chosen a Member of the House of Representatives?
A. Twenty-five years old.

Q49. May a person be chosen who has just come into the United States, and who is a subject of some other country (that means, who is bound to obey the laws of some other country)?
A. No. Any person, to be chosen a Member of our House of Representatives, must either have been born in the United States, or must have been *naturalized* seven years before he is chosen.

Q50. Naturalized? What does that mean?
A. A person who was born in another country and who comes to live in this, is not owned as a citizen of the United States till he has lived among us a certain time; and then, (after knowing something of our laws and customs) has taken a solemn oath to obey the government. He is then admitted as a citizen of our republic. This is called his *naturalization*; and when once *naturalized*, he is allowed to choose the rulers, and do all other things, the same as if he had been born among us.

Q51. May the people of one State choose a person who is an inhabitant of another State to be a Member of the House of Representatives?
A. No; he must live in the State where he is chosen.

Q52. How many persons may be chosen by each State, as Members of the House of Representatives?
A. The number of Representatives of any State is in proportion to the number of people in that State. At present every forty thousand people send one Representative; but this has been, and may be, altered, with the increase of the number of people.

Q53. Some of the States have large numbers of slaves living in them, and others have many Indians; are these counted in making up the forty thousand?
A. No; three-fifths of the number of slaves is allowed, that is every five slaves are counted as if they were three free persons: those Indians who pay taxes, (that is, who pay money for the expenses of governing and defending us) are counted; those who do not pay taxes are not counted. *

Q54. How is it known what number of people each State contains?
A. Certain persons are appointed to count the people and take a written list of them. Such a counting is called a *census*, and it takes place once every ten years.

Q55. When the Members of the House of Representatives meet to make the laws, are they all equal, or does any one preside over them?
A. They choose one of their own number, whose duty it is to preside over them while they are met to do business, and to see that they proceed in a regular and orderly manner in doing their public duty. He is called their *Speaker*. They also choose a person who is not one of their own number to keep a written account, from day to day, of all that is done by them while assembled. That written account is called a *Journal* of the House of Representatives, and the person who keeps it is called the *Clerk of the House*. They also choose another person who is called their *Sergeant-at-Arms*, and who may, when so ordered by the House, seize any Member who disobeys the rules, or who is charged by the House with any crime, and imprison him. They also choose another person as their *Door Keeper*, who is to take care that no person be admitted into the hall where the Representatives are sitting, but such as are permitted by law. These several persons, thus chosen, are called the Officers of the House of Representatives, and remain in office two years.

Q56. Who chooses the Members of the SENATE OF THE UNITED STATES? **
A. The Legislature of each State chooses the Senators for that State.

Q57. How many Senators may there be?

---

* See notes on pages 48-52 after Catechism. It is critical that you read all of the editorial notes. You may write to us with your comments or criticisms and help us to improve this work in a later edition.

** Compare Article I, Section 3, Clause 1, of the Constitution (found on page 70) with the Seventeenth Amendment (found on page 88), to see how this provision has been amended.

A. Two from each state.

Q58. When a citizen is chosen by the Legislature of his own State to be a Member of the Senate of the United States, how long does he continue such?
A. For six years. If he dies before the expiration of that time, or resigns his office, (that is, if he declares it to be his wish not to be a Senator any longer) another is appointed in his place.

Q59. Are all the Senators chosen at the same time, as Members of the House of Representatives are?
A. No. Only one third are chosen at once - two years afterward another third is chosen - and two years after that, another third, so that every two years one third part of the Senators go out of office; but the same persons may again be chosen if the Legislatures who chose them before wish to send them again; if not, they send others in their place.

Q60. How old must a person be before he can be chosen a Senator of the United States?
A. Thirty years old.

Q61. Can he be chosen if he has not been born in the United States?
A. Yes, if he has become a citizen by being naturalized, and has been a citizen for nine years.

Q62. Can a Senator for one State be chosen by the Legislature of another State?
A. No. The Legislature of each State must choose its own Senators, from persons residing in its own bounds.

Q63. Does the Senate choose a *Speaker*, as the House of Representatives does?
A. No. The person who is chosen by the people to be Vice President of the United States, is made, by the Constitution, President of the Senate; his duties are like those of the Speaker of the House of Representatives, except that he is obliged to keep order in debate. Their other officers are the same in all respects, as those of the House of Representatives, and are chosen by the Senators in the same manner.

Q64. Do the Senators ever sit as Judges?
A. Yes. When any civil officer of the United States (that is, not an officer of the army), is guilty of a violation of his public duty, he is accused, or charged, by the House of Representatives, and tried by the Senate. Such an accusation is called *Impeachment*.

Q65. What do you mean by his being tried by the Senate?
A. The Senators take a solemn oath that they will carefully attend to the proof that shall be brought before them, and according to that proof declare the accused

person innocent or guilty, as the case may be. The House of Representatives appoint some of their own Members to lay the proof before the Senate, and afterwards the accused person lays before them the proofs in his defence; when both have been heard, the Members of the Senate vote, that is, each one declares his opinion; and if two thirds of all the Senators who are present declare the accused person to be guilty, he is adjudged guilty; if not, he is declared not guilty.

Q66. Cannot the Senate, in like manner, *impeach*, that is, solemnly charge an officer before the House of Representatives?
A. No. None can bring an impeachment but the House of Representatives, and none can try an impeachment but the Senate.

Q67. What is the consequence if the Senate declare an officer of the United States to be guilty?
A. He may be turned out of office, and prevented from ever again holding any office of honor, trust, or profit, under the United States government.

Q68. May he be further punished?
A. Not by the Senate. He may afterwards be tried before a Court of Law, and punished in the same manner as any other criminal for offences against the law.

Q69. May ever the President of the United States be thus impeached and punished?
A. Yes. In this free and happy country no man is so great as to be above the law. The laws are supreme; to them all persons, from the President of the United States to the poorest and the meanest beggar, must alike submit. This is our glory. Let every youthful American exult that he has no master but the law; let him mark the man who would change this happy state of things as an enemy of his country; and above all let him remember that as soon as he himself breaks the law, he becomes himself that enemy. Whoever violates the law helps to weaken its force, and, as far as he disobeys, does what in him lies to destroy it; but he who honors and obeys the law strengthens the law, and thereby helps to preserve the freedom and happiness of his country. In some governments it is held that "the king can do no wrong;" here we know no king but the law, no monarch but the constitution; we hold that every man may do wrong; the higher he is in office, the more reason there is that he be obliged to answer for his conduct; and a great officer, if treacherous, is a great criminal, so that he ought to be made to suffer a great and exemplary punishment.

Q70. How often does Congress meet?
A. It must meet once, at least, in every year; but may meet oftener if necessary.

Q71. Is any day fixed for its meeting?
A. Yes; the first Monday in December; but it has the power to alter that to some other fixed day. When Congress ceases to meet, it is said to *Adjourn*.

Q72. Suppose all the members of the Senate, or all the members of the House of Representatives do not attend a meeting, can those who do attend make laws without them?
A. If more than one half are present, they have in most cases the power to do whatever the whole number could have done. More than one half are called a *Majority*, less than one half are called a *Minority*. As many as are necessary to do business are called a *Quorum*.

Q73. Supposing less than one half should attend, can they do nothing?
A. Yes, they have the power to send for the others and compel them to attend. If they do not choose to do this, they have power to adjourn till the next day; (that is, they may separate after agreeing to meet the next day;) and so they may continue to do till a *Quorum* shall be present to do business.

Q74. Are there any fixed rules for doing business in Congress?
A. Certainly, everything is done by settled rules, called *Rules of Order*.

Q75. Who settles what these rules shall be?
A. The Rules for the Senate are made by the Senate; the Rules for the House of Representatives are made by the House of Representatives. Each House has power to alter its own Rules of order; or to suspend them, that is to say, a particular rule may be disobeyed for a certain time; after which it is again in force.

Q76. Suppose a Member refuses to attend, or behaves, when he does attend, in a disorderly manner?
A. He may be punished in any way the other Members think proper.

Q77. May he be even expelled from the House? that is, turned out of it?
A. Yes, but not unless two thirds of all the Members think he deserves it.

Q78. You said that the Clerk of the House of Representatives keeps a written *Journal* of all that is done in that House; is a Journal kept in like manner by the Secretary of the Senate?
A. Yes.

Q79. Are these Journals published? that is, printed and sold?
A. Yes; excepting such part as either House of Congress may think proper to keep secret for a time, when the public good requires it.

Q80. Do Congress ever sit in secret?
A. Yes. Whenever they are engaged in business which it will be better for the public good to keep secret for a time, they close their doors. At other times they

sit in public, and every body who can get into the gallery may see and hear all that is done.

Q81. Does the Journal shew how each Member voted in every case that came to be considered?
A. No. But if one fifth of the Members present when any measure is proposed, require that the names of those who voted for and against it, be put down in the Journal, it must be done.

Q82. After Congress has met, may either House adjourn (that is, cease to meet) for more than three days at a time, without consent of the other House?
A. No.

Q83. Do the two Houses, that is, the Senate and House of Representatives, meet in the same building?
A. Yes.

Q84. May either House remove to any other place?
A. No, not unless the other House removes too.

Q85. Do the Members of Congress receive any thing for doing the business of the public?
A. Their chief and best reward is the honor of serving their country; but as many of them cannot afford to leave their own business so often and so long without having the loss in some measure made up to them, the Constitution says that they shall be allowed a compensation to be ascertained by law, and paid out of the Treasury of the United States.

Q86. Who fixes the rate of compensation, that is, how much the Members shall have?
A. It is fixed by Congress.

Q87. Ought they to be allowed to fix their own wages?
A. It cannot be avoided; the rate must be fixed by law, and there is none who have power to make law for this country but the Congress only.

Q88. May Members of congress be arrested, (that is, seized by a sheriff or constable) for debts they owe, while they are attending to their public duty?
A. Their duty is of so much value to us all that the Constitution will not allow them to be arrested while going and returning from their home to the place where Congress meets, nor while they are attending there, except in three cases.

Q89. What are these?
A. If they have been guilty of treason, felony, or breach of the peace.

Q90. When is a person guilty of *treason*?

A. When he makes war against the United States - (that is, when he endeavors by force to overturn or to resist the Government,) or when he helps or comforts others who are making war against them. [But this must be proved by at least two witnesses, who have both seen him do some act of treason. The crime is punished in any way Congress thinks fit; and they have determined that it shall be punishable by death.]

Q91. If Members of Congress while engaged in debate, that is, in arguing about any law that is proposed to be made, shall say any thing offensive to another Member, may he be sued for it by the other in a Court of Law?

A. No; (lest this should destroy the freedom of debate, and make the Members afraid of speaking their thoughts with honesty and plainness in matters for the public good,) a Member cannot be called to account in any other place for any thing he says upon the floor of Congress.

Q92. May Members of Congress be appointed to any civil office under the United States?

A. Not while they continue to be Members; if they are appointed to any office and wish to accept the appointment, they must give up their seats in Congress; nor can they be chosen Members again while they hold the office.

Q93. Supposing Congress create any new office, (that is, appoint some public duty to be done and allow the person who does it a compensation) or shall increase the pay before allowed for doing the duties of any office, that is already established, - may any Member of the Congress which did this be appointed to such office?

A. No, not till the whole time for which he was chosen a Member shall have expired.

Q94. How do Congress proceed in making the laws?

A. A Member usually proposes that some other Members, called a *Committee*, shall consider whether it will not be proper to make a law for some particular matter, which he explains. If a majority of the Members think it will be best to consider of the matter, they order certain Members to do so. These Members, or *Committee*, meet together, and having considered the proposal, determine whether it is proper to advise the Members of the House to make a law respecting it. If they think it is they put down in writing the words of such a law as it will be best to make. This writing is called a *Bill*. They then return to the House, and either in writing or by word of mouth, declare what they have done, and state the reasons for it. Such a statement is called a Committee's *Report*. The *Bill* is then read twice. The Member who first proposed the matter now farther proposes, (or *Moves*, as it is called) that this *Bill* be considered by all the Members. If this is agreed to, the Bill is then taken under consideration. Every Member has an opportunity to propose such alterations in it, as he pleases; and every Member may give reasons why such a law ought or ought not to be made.

If any alterations are made, the Bill as altered is written over again and read a third time; when, after full consideration, it is *Passed*, that is, finally agreed to.

Q95. Is it now a law?

A. By no means. The Bill thus passed by one House is sent to the other House. There it is again considered, and, if the House thinks proper, is farther altered. It is then returned to the House where it began. If this House disapproves of the alterations made by the other, it sends the Bill back, that House may give up alterations - but if they will not give them up, then a *Committee of Conference* is appointed; that is, certain Members are sent from each House to meet together, and try to bring the matter into such a form that both Houses will agree to it; - if they succeed, and the Houses agree, the Bill is then *Engrossed*, (that is, copied in a fair hand) on parchment, and signed by the President and Secretary of the Senate, and by the Speaker and Clerk of the House of Representatives.

Q96. Is it now a law?

A. Not yet. The engrossed Bill is then sent to the President of the United States for his approbation; if he approves it, he signs and returns it; the *Bill* then is called an ACT, and becomes the law of the land.

Q97. How if he does not approve it?

A. If he does not approve it, he must return the Bill together with his objections, in writing, to the House in which it began; that House must copy the whole of these objections into their Journal and then consider the Bill once more. When they have done this, if two thirds of that House shall agree to pass the Bill, they must send it, together with the President's objections to it, to the other House. There the Bill must, in like manner, be re-considered; and if two thirds of this House also agree to pass it, it becomes a Law. But in all such cases, the names of all the Members of each House who voted for and against the Bill, must be put down in the Journals.

Q98. Suppose the President of the United States should neglect to sign and return a Bill sent to him by Congress?

A. If he does not sign or return any Bill within ten days after it is sent to him, (not counting Sundays) it becomes a Law, unless in that time Congress shall have ceased to sit.

Q99. Is not this a better way of making the laws of a Country, than either of those we first considered?

A. It is hard to conceive how greater care could be taken that no wicked, unjust, oppressive, hasty, or unwise Law should pass. There is full time to consider whatever is proposed; such fair opportunity to oppose it, if wrong, and improve it, if imperfect; so many persons, and from so wide a space of country must agree in approving it, that it is scarcely possible any thing very injurious can be enacted; or, at least, if it is, that a different form of Government would have prevented it. *

Q100. Are there not some evils which attend this mode?
A. Nothing of human contrivance is wholly free from some defect or other; and in time of war, when the public danger is great, and it is needful that Government should act, not only wisely, but rapidly; some disadvantage may be found to arise from so deliberate a method of passing every Law. But it is far better to put up with this, than to lose the precious blessing of so free and safe a mode of Legislation.

Q101. You have said that no Laws can be made for the United States, but by Congress; may Congress make any Laws they please?
A. No. Their power is limited by the Constitution; that is, they have no power, but what the Constitution says they have. It must always be remembered, that the States, when they united to form the General Government, had full power to govern themselves; and that they gave up only a *part of their power*, for the general welfare. Whatever power, therefore, is not given by the Constitution, to the General Government, still belongs either to the State Governments, or to the people of the United States.

Q102. What power is given to Congress, by the Constitution?
A. Congress has power to do the following things: -It may "lay and collect Taxes, Duties, Imposts and Excises."

Q103. What do you mean by these different terms? What is a Tax?
A. A Tax means a sum of money which the people are directed to pay, to support the Government, and defence of the Country. *

Q104. What are Duties?
A. Duties are sums of money, which must be paid by persons who bring goods of any kind from another country, into the United States, and which are in proportion to the quantity or value of such goods. It is paid at certain places called Custom-houses, and is sent from these to the Treasury of the United States.

Q105. What are Imposts?
A. Imposts are sums of money which must be paid to the Government, by persons owning vessels, which enter the harbors of the United States, in proportion to the size of the vessels. An Impost is a duty on vessels.

Q106. What are Excises?

---

* See Editor's Notes on Pages 48-52 after the Catechism. It is critical that you read all of the notes. You are encouraged to write us with your criticisms and comments and help us to improve this work in a later edition.

A. Excises are sums of money which must be paid to the Government, by persons who make certain articles within the United States, in proportion to the quantity or value of the articles manufactured.

Q107. What do you mean by *laying* these, and what by *collecting* them?
A. Laying a Tax, &c., is determining how much it shall be; and collecting a Tax, &c., is obliging people to pay it.

Q108. Could any Government long exist without this power?
A. No. Every Government must have large sums of money, to use for the public good, and this is the proper way of getting it.

Q109. Ought people to complain of having to pay Taxes and Duties?
A. Certainly not; because they all receive the benefit. If nobody would pay Taxes, nobody could be defended by armies, fleets, or forts; nobody could be paid for making or executing laws; the whole country would soon be without law, safety or order; and we should all be miserable. Whoever, therefore, cheats the Government of its duties, does in reality cheat himself and his neighbor, and acts like the enemy of his country. *

Q110. May one part of the United States be required to pay at a greater rate than the rest?
A. No; "all Duties, Imposts, and Excises must be uniform throughout the United States."

Q111. What other power has Congress?
A. "To borrow money on the credit of the United States." *

Q112. What do you mean by that expression, "on the credit of the United States?"
A. It means that the people of the United States are bound to pay whatever money Congress borrows for their use. [Such money is called a *Loan*; and whoever lends it to the Government, receives a printed paper, acknowledging that such a sum has been lent, and promising to pay a smaller sum yearly, as *Interest* for the use of it. Such printed certificates are called *Stock*; they may be bought and sold the same as any other article, - and whoever holds them when the interest becomes due, may demand, and must receive, it. If the printed paper promises to pay six dollars a year for every hundred dollars borrowed, it is called "United States six per cent Stock;" if it promises to pay four dollars a year for every hundred, then it is called "United States four per cent stock."]

Q113. What other power does Congress possess?

---

* See Editor's Notes on Pages 48-52 after the Catechism. It is critical that you read all of the notes. You are encouraged to write us with your criticisms and comments and help us to improve this work in a later edition.

A. It may make rules according to which the Commerce of the citizens of the United States with other nations (that is the exchange of our goods for theirs, or for money, by means of vessels or other conveyances) shall be carried on; also the commerce of one of the states with another, and that of the different states, or of the United States, with the Indian tribes. [Some persons believe that the power to regulate Commerce among the several states includes the power to make Roads and Canals from one state to another; others deny this.]

Q114. What is the next power given to Congress by the Constitution?
A. You recollect what was before said about *naturalization*, which means the admitting of a foreigner (that is, a native of some other country) to become a citizen of the United States: - Congress has power to make one uniform rule according to which this shall be done throughout the country. It may also make uniform Laws for the whole Union on the subject of Bankruptcy.

Q115. What is bankruptcy?
A. When a man has not money or goods enough to pay his debts he is a *Bankrupt*; and the being in that situation is *Bankruptcy*. The object of Laws on this subject is to compel such a man to give up all he has got to the people he owes, and to fix the terms on which he may be set free from the debts he cannot pay.

Q116. What else may Congress do?
A. It may coin money; that is it may mark or stamp certain pieces of metal in a way which shall make them pass, in buying and selling, at a set value. It may also fix what shall be the value of the coin that has been marked or stamped in any other country, when it is used in the United States. It may likewise declare one uniform size for the weights and measures used throughout our Country.*

Q117. May any persons who please coin money?
A. No, none but those employed to do so by Congress; (they work at a place called the *mint*.)

Q118. If any other person shall coin money in his own name, or shall stamp it so as to resemble that coined at the mint, or that which though coined in other countries, is allowed to pass as money in the United States, (called "*Current coin*"), may he be punished?
A. Yes; it is a crime, called *counterfeiting*, and may be punished in any manner Congress shall appoint.

Q119. Suppose they counterfeit not the money of the United States, but the *stock* issued by the Government?

---

* See notes on pages 48-52 after Catechism. It is critical that you read all of the editorial notes. You are encouraged to write us with your criticisms and comments and help us to improve this work in a later edition.

A. They are punished the same as if they had counterfeited money.

Q120. What other power belongs to Congress?
A. They may "establish Post Offices and Post Roads."

Q121. What is a Post Office?
A. A place where Letters carried from one part of the country to another, at the expense of the United States, are received and delivered.

Q122. And what is a Post Road?
A. A road on which the bag containing these letters (called the *mail*), is carried.

Q123. What is meant by *establishing* these?
A. Making a law which directs where the Post Offices shall be, and by what roads the mail shall be carried. Some persons say that it includes a power to erect buildings for post offices, and to make roads where they are wanted; others deny this.

Q124. Has Congress any farther powers?
A. It may grant what are termed Patent Rights and Copy Rights.

Q125. What does this mean?
A. When a person has found out some new and useful contrivance, Congress may give him an exclusive right to make and sell what he has contrived, for a certain number of years; during that time nobody else may make or sell that article without leave from the man who contrived it, and if they do they are liable to be punished. This is called a *Patent Right*. Whoever writes a book may also have the exclusive right to print and sell it for a certain time; this is called a *Copy Right*.

Q126. Can Congress erect *Courts*? that is, make a Law directing that a Judge shall sit at certain places, at certain times, before whom Causes or Criminals shall be tried?
A. Yes, it may appoint as many Courts as it thinks fit; but they must be inferior to the great Court of the country, called the *Supreme Court of the United States*.

Q127. Can it punish *Piracy*? that is, robbery committed at sea?
A. Yes, and all other crimes committed there; it can also punish offences against *the law of nations*.

Q128. What do you mean by the "law of nations"?
A. I mean those rules which are agreed upon among all nations (except those who are savages) to regulate their conduct towards each other.

Q129. Has Congress any other power?

A. Yes, it has one most solemn and important power, the power of Declaring War between the United States and any other nation.

Q130. When Congress has declared the United States to be at war with any particular country, can any of the citizens of the United States remain at peace with that nation?
A. No; however much they may dislike the war, or love the nation against whom it is declared, all must, when required, aid in it, by their money or their services, and bring it as soon as possible to a successful end. If they attempt to aid the enemy, or forcibly hinder the success of the war, they commit treason.

Q131. When the United States have cause of complaint against another nation, and yet do not wish at once to go to war, is there any other measure they can take to compel that nation to do them justice?
A. Yes. Congress may "issue Letters of Marque, and Reprisal."

Q132. What are they?
A. They are certain public letters directed to merchants of the United States, who have been injured, and have been refused redress, permitting them forcible to take vessels belonging to the offending nation, sufficient to make up the loss; but this must be done only according to certain Rules, fixed by Congress.

Q133. You say Congress may declare War; can they raise Armies; that is can they hire soldiers to fight for our country?
A. They can; and pay, clothe, and feed them, at the public expense.

Q134. Can they make a law, setting apart money enough at one time, to pay and support the army for more than two years?
A. No, not at one time; lest a wicked Congress might, by keeping up an army, remain in power beyond the time for which they were chosen, and so destroy the liberty of their country.

Q135. Why was the time limited to two years?
A. Because every two years a new Congress may be chosen.

Q136. Can Congress in like manner, provide and maintain a Navy? that is, buy or build ships of war; and hire, clothe, and feed men to navigate and fight them?
A. Yes; and make Rules to govern both Army and Navy.

Q137. Has the Country no other defence to depend upon but hired soldiers?
A. Yes, the people themselves, who are of proper age to bear the fatigues and hardships of War, are obliged to bear arms and defend their Country when need requires; they are called the *Militia*.

Q138. When may they be called out, to do this?

A. When they are wanted, to enforce the laws; to overcome any of their fellow citizens, who are so foolish and wicked as to rebel against our free and excellent form of government; or to meet and drive out an enemy who invades; that is, forcibly enters any part of our Country.

Q139. But as the great mass of the people are ignorant of the art of War, how is this to be done?
A. Congress has power to provide for their being taught, by collecting and arranging them in companies, and regiments, under their own officers; supplying them with arms, and causing them to be properly exercised in their use.

Q140. May Congress command them, or are they to be commanded by their own State Governments?
A. The President may command so many of them as are employed in the service of the United States, the rest are commanded by the States.

Q141. Who appoints the Officers of the Militia?
A. The State Government; they also *train*, that is, exercise and instruct the men; but this must be done according to Rules fixed by Congress.

Q142. Have you mentioned all the powers of Congress?
A. No; they have the power to make *all* the Laws for a certain District, not more than ten miles square, where Congress meets, and where the Chief Officers of Government reside. This is called the Seat of Government.

Q143. Has this District no Legislature of its own choice, as the States have?
A. No.

Q144. Is it a part of any State?
A. No. It consists of territory, which the States have given up, for the express purpose that it might be the Seat of Government. The territory at present used for this purpose, is called the *District of Columbia*; and has been ceded, (that is, given up) by the States of Maryland and Virginia, within which it before lay.

Q145. Is there any other place in the United States, which is thus ruled by Congress alone?
A. Yes - all Forts, Magazines, (that is, places where powder and other things used by an army are laid up) Arsenals, (that is, buildings where arms are kept) and Dock-yards; (that is, places where vessels of war are built) which belong to the United States, are governed, not by the Legislatures of the States in which they may be, but by the General Government alone.

Q146. What other power is conferred by the Constitution upon the Congress of the United States?

A.   A very large and general authority, "to make all laws which shall be necessary and proper for carrying into execution the foregoing powers," (that is, all the powers of which we have been speaking) "and all other powers vested by the Constitution in the Government of the United States, or in any department or officer thereof." Thus, for example, when the Constitution says, that Congress may coin money, that gives Congress power to make all the laws necessary to determine what the coin shall be - how they shall be marked) of what metal they shall be made - what shall be their weight - what shall be their value - where they shall be made - what buildings shall be erected for the purpose - how many persons shall be employed - what their duty shall be - what pay they shall receive - what account they shall keep - what security they shall give, and how they shall be punished if they neglect their duty. It is the same with every other power given by the Constitution; if its execution requires a hundred different laws, Congress may pass them all. *

Q147. May slaves be imported, that is, brought into the United States?
A. No, whoever engages in the slave trade is a pirate.

Q148. May slaves be held, that is, owned, and made to work - by citizens of the United States? **
A. Yes.

Q149. If they escape from one State into another, may the State into which they flee set them at liberty?
A. No.

150. Suppose any American citizen is seized and put into prison, may he be kept there as long as those who seized him think fit?
A. No; he may get a *writ of Habeas Corpus*.

Q151. What is that?
A. It is a command from Court, by which the jailor is forced to allow the prisoner to be brought up before a Judge, that the cause of his being put in prison may be examined into, in order, that if there is no law to keep him there, he may immediately be set at liberty.

Q152. Must this command be given whenever it is applied for?
A. Yes, except at certain times, when this privilege is *suspended*; (that is, interrupted for a time, but not taken away).

---

* See notes on pages 48-52 after Catechism. It is critical that you read all of the editorial notes. You may write to us with your comments or criticisms and help us to improve this work in a later edition.
** See the Thirteenth and Fouteenth Amendments and Editor's Notes on Q53.

Q153. When may this right of having a writ of Habeas Corpus, which belongs by the Constitution to every citizen, be suspended?

A. Only in cases of rebellion by our own citizens, or invasion of the country by an enemy; when the public danger is so great as to require persons to be kept in prison, who might otherwise have been set at liberty. As soon as this extreme danger is past, the right of *Habeas Corpus* must be immediately restored.

Q154. Is this a very great and important privilege, and ought all Americans to guard it with the greatest care?

A. It is one of the greatest rights of a freeman -- and Americans must never surrender it, under any pretext, if they value and would preserve their liberty. *

Q155. May a man's children be punished by law for his offence?

A. In some countries, where a man has been guilty of treason, (that is making war against the Government) a law is passed called a *bill of attainder*, by which his children are prevented from being heirs to him or to any other person; and, if he belonged to what in those countries is called the nobility, and his children would have belonged to it too, they are prevented; nor can they nor their children, nor their children's children, recover this privilege, till an act is passed for that purpose. No such law can be made in this country; it is expressly forbidden by the Constitution.

Q156. May a citizen of the United States be punished for doing what, when he did it, was not forbidden by any law, but against which a law was passed *afterwards?*

A. No. A law that attempts to punish actions that were done before the law was made, is called an "*ex-post-facto* law." This also is expressly forbidden by the Constitution.

Q157. When a direct tax is laid, that is, when Congress order that a certain sum of money must be paid by each citizen, for the public use, what is the rule by which it is to be collected? *

A The census or public counting of the people.

Q158. May any money be required to be paid on goods exported, (that is, carried out), from any of the States?

A. No.

Q159. May any law be passed giving to the *ports* of one State, (that is, the places where vessels arrive and depart with goods) preference over those of another, so that goods coming to some ports shall have less duties to pay to Government than the same goods coming to other ports?

---

* See notes on pages 48-52 after Catechism. It is critical you read all of the editorial notes. You are encouraged to write us with your criticisms and comments and help us to improve this work in a later edition.

A.　No.

Q160.　May vessels coming from sea with goods which they wish to deliver in one State, be obliged to land those goods, or to *enter* them, that is, give an account of them at the Custom-house, or to pay the duties on them in another State?

A.　No.

Q161.　When a vessel leaves the ports of one State with goods which she is carrying to sea, can she be obliged to *clear* those goods, that is, give account of them at the Custom-house, in another State?

A.　No; each State may carry on its own commerce without the interference of any other State.

Q162.　In what way can the money of the United States be drawn out of the *Treasury?* (or place where it is kept)

A.　It can be drawn out only by authority of Congress; and such a law is called an *Appropriation*.

Q163.　Must a full account be kept of all moneys received into the Treasury, and paid out of it; and must this account be published, that is printed and sold from time to time?

A.　Yes.

Q164.　You said that in some countries part of the people are called Nobility; what does that mean?

A.　Almost all of Europe was once under the power of Rome, and formed part of what was called the Roman Empire. This Empire was attacked, overrun, and at last conquered entirely, by a hardy set of people who came from the north in vast numbers. These people were commanded by their chiefs or kings; and when the countries which they invaded gave up fighting, and yielded every thing to the conquerors, the whole of the land was divided into portions and given by the king to his chief officers, who divided it again among their followers. These great officers were called by various names or *titles;* as Dukes, Earls, Counts, &c. and when they died, their oldest sons were called by the same *titles;* which continued in this manner to descend in certain great and rich families. It is these families which are now known in most countries of Europe as *Nobles,* or *Nobility*--and they have great privileges over the other citizens.

Q165.　Can any families be thus distinguished from the rest in this Republic?

A.　No; no title of Nobility can be granted here. The only titles, among us, are those which mark a person's grade in the army or navy, or his office in the State.

Q166.　May any citizen of the United States receive a title of nobility from the king, or prince, or government of any other country?

A. The Government does not interfere with *private* persons; but no person holding an office of profit or trust under the republic can accept of either a title, a sum of money as salary, an office, or even a present, from any such prince or government, without the express consent of Congress.

Q167. Why is this?
A. To guard against any foreign prince getting influence over those who are in power among us, by bribes of any kind; a title would be a better bribe to some men than money.

Q168. You said that when the states entered into that agreement by which they set up a General Government over them all, they had each a perfect right to govern themselves as free, sovereign and independent States; and that they gave up a part of their power to the General Government, and kept the rest of it in their own hands. What are the powers which they gave up?
A. The power of *making treaties*, (that is bargains or agreements with other nations) *alliances,* (that is agreements with some other country, that the two shall help each other, in something they wish to accomplish, or in avoiding some common danger,) and *confederations*, (that is agreements among several different countries, that they shall all join together in some object for their common benefit.) None of these acts can now be performed by any one of the states, separately, but must be done only for the whole by the General Government.

Q169. What other powers did they give up?
A. The right to *grant letters of marque and reprisal*; the right to *coin money;* -- (both have been explained) -- the right *to emit bills of credit;* (that is, to issue printed promises to pay certain sums of money on the credit of the state, the same as a Bank issues Bank notes) to make any thing but gold and silver a lawful tender in the payment of debts.

Q170. What does that mean?
A. When one man owes another, and goes to him and offers him money to the full amount of his debt, that is called a *tender* (or offer) and if the money is such as the law says shall pass, it is a *lawful tender;* and if the man refuses it, he can never sue the other for that debt, nor is the debtor obliged to pay it. Now, though money is commonly made of gold and silver, yet sometimes a Government may make a law by which certain printed notes are to pass the same as gold or silver; and after such a law, that kind of printed notes are a *lawful tender* to pay debts with. (This kind of paper was issued by Congress in our revolution.) The states, by the Constitution, gave up the power to do this, and now it can be done by the General Government only.*

---

* See notes on pages 48-52 after Catechism. It is critical that you read all of the editor's notes. You are encouraged to write us with your criticisms and comments and help us to improve this work in a late edition.

Q171. Did the states give up any other power?
A. They are forbidden by the Constitution, in the same manner that Congress is, to pass any bill of attainder, or ex-post-facto law, or grant any title of nobility, nor can they make any law which shall "impair the obligation of contracts."

Q172. What does that mean?
A. It means that when a bargain has been made between two parties, by which one agrees and binds himself to do some particular thing not *then* forbidden by law, the state in which this agreement, or *contract*, was made shall not afterwards make any law by which the person who has bound himself shall be set free from any part of that bargain without the consent of the other party, with whom he made the contract.

Q173. What else are the states forbidden to do?
A. They cannot lay any duty on exports or imports.

Q174. May they not lay enough duty to pay for the expenses of collecting the duties laid by Congress?
A. Yes, but no more; and if more is received than is wanted for this use, it must be paid into the Treasury of the United States.

Q175. May any of the States lay a tonnage tax; that is, require a sum of money to be paid by every vessel entering any of the harbors in that State?
A. No.

Q176. May they keep soldiers whom they pay, in time of peace?
A. No.

Q177. May they keep ships of war, in time of peace?
A. No.

Q178. May one State enter into an agreement with any other nation?
A. No.

Q179. May they make war?
A. No; not unless an enemy has entered their bounds, or is in such danger of entering, that there is no time to wait for the aid of the General Government.

Q180. Why did the States give up all these powers?
A. Because they could better be protected by one powerful Government ruling over them all united than they could have been, if they had remained separate; and, if they would have such a Government, they must consent each to give up a part of

their own power, in order to make it: if the General Government had no power, it would be of no use. *

Q181. Who *executes* the laws which Congress have made, that is, who takes care that every body shall obey the laws?
A. The President of the United States.

Q182. Can he make the law?
A. Not at all. These two powers, of *making* law, and *executing* law, are kept by the Constitution, entirely separate; the power that makes the law cannot execute it, and the power that executes the law cannot make it. (The one of these powers is called the *Legislative*, and the other is called the *Executive* power.)

Q183. Is there any advantage in this?
A. Certainly; it is a great safeguard of freedom; because, if the one makes *oppressive* laws, the other may refuse to execute them; or, if the one wishes to do *tyrannical* acts, the other may refuse to make the law for them.

Q184. How does any man become the president of the United States?
A. He is elected (chosen) by the people of the United States.

Q185. How is this done; do the people themselves at once choose the President?
A. No; this might lead to great confusion. But the people choose the Legislatures of the different States, those Legislatures appoint electors, and those electors choose the President.

Q186. Explain this more particularly.
A. You know what is meant by the Legislatures of the States; they consist of persons chosen in each State to make the State laws. These persons, when met together, appoint, in any way they think proper, a number of persons who are called Electors, because they afterwards choose the President.

Q187. How many of these Electors of President are appointed in each State?
A. As many as the state has members in both Houses of Congress. For instance; a state which is entitled to two Senators and eight members of the House of Representatives must appoint ten electors of President; a state which has two Senators and twenty members of the House of Representatives, must appoint twenty-two electors.

Q188. May any person they please be appointed an elector?

---

* See Editor's Notes on Pages 48-52 after the Catechism. It is critical that you read all of the notes. You are encouraged to write us with your criticisms and comments and help us to improve this work in a later edition.

A. Not every person may; Senators of the United States, members of the House of Representatives, and all persons who hold any office of trust or profit under the United States, are incapable of being electors of the President.

Q189. Why?
A. For fear any President of the United States might use improper means to get himself chosen again when his time of service should expire. The President has frequent opportunities to see the members of Congress and persuade them; and as he himself has the appointment of most persons who hold offices, he might threaten to remove, or promise to keep them in their places, and thus destroy their freedom of election.

Q190. How do these electors proceed?
A. The electors appointed by each state meet in the states that appointed them, and vote *by ballot* for the President, and for another officer called the *Vice President* of the United States. The electors all meet on one and the same day in their several states; the day is fixed by Congress.

Q191. What do you mean by *voting by ballot*?
A. When it is wished to conceal the manner in which each particular person voted, and yet to know what is the opinion of the greater number of voters, the voters instead of *speaking* their minds, put each a piece of folded paper into a box; these papers are called *ballots*, and when all have voted, these ballots are examined and counted.

Q192. May both the persons whom the electors of any state vote for, as President and Vice President, be natives of that state in which they are voted for?
A. No; only one of them; the other must be a native of some other state.

Q193. How do they distinguish which of the persons is voted for as President and which as Vice President?
A. The ballots are taken separately, on different pieces of paper, and it is besides written on the ballot whether the person is voted for as one or the other. Separate lists are kept in which they put down the names of all the persons who are voted for, either as President or as Vice President, and the number of votes given for each; these lists are signed by the electors, and then sealed up and sent to the seat of government directed to the President of the Senate. For the greater security, two copies are made, one of them is sent by the mail, and another by a messenger, sent for the express purpose of carrying it.

Q194. What does the President of the Senate do with these lists?
A. He opens them in the presence of the Senate and the House of Representatives, who are all met in one hall to be present when the votes are counted. Each House appoints some of its own members who unite in a committee and count all the votes; then the person having the greatest number of votes for President is

declared to be President, and he who has the most votes for Vice President is declared Vice President of the United States.

Q195. Suppose no one person has a majority (that is more than half) of all the votes for President, is the person who has the most votes considered as chosen?
A. No.

Q196. What is done in that case?
A. The House of Representatives immediately proceed to choose, by ballot, from those persons, not more than three, who stand the highest on the list of votes for President, one to be President of the United States.

Q197. Are they bound to choose the person who has the most votes?
A. No; they may take either one of those three persons who have the most votes.

Q198. Do they vote, on this occasion, in a different manner from what they do on all other occasions?
A. Yes; in choosing the President they vote, not by single members, but by States; that is, each State has one vote only, whether its Representatives are many or few; and a majority of the whole number of States is necessary to a choice.

Q199. Must all the States vote?
A. All may vote if they are present and desire it; but if only two thirds of the States vote, the election is good.

Q200. Suppose the House of Representatives cannot, or do not, choose any one, must there be no President?
A. In that case, the Vice President must perform the duty of President.

Q201. If neither of the persons voted for by the Electors as Vice President has a majority of all their votes, what is done?
A. The Senate then chooses one of the two persons who have the most votes. A majority of the whole number of Senators is necessary to the choice, but two thirds of their number is sufficient to vote.

Q202. May any person be chosen President of the United States?
A. Not every person; none may be chosen unless he has been born in the United States, or was a citizen when the Constitution was agreed to, nor can such a one be chosen if he is less than thirty-five years old, or if he has not resided within the United States for fourteen years.

Q203. May any person be chosen Vice President?
A. No one may be chosen as Vice President who is forbidden by the above rule to be chosen as President.

Q204. Suppose the President of the United States should die, or should be put out of office, or should resign his office, or should from any cause be unable to do the duties which belong to it, what is to be done?
A. His duties must then be performed by the Vice President.

Q205. But suppose the same thing should have happened to the Vice President?
A. Then the Congress must declare by law who shall perform the duties till another President is chosen, or till the President is again able to perform them himself.

Q206. Does the President receive any thing for his services?
A. The honor of filling so high and honorable a station by the choice of a great and free people, and the glory of leaving his name in their history as the faithful friend and father of his country, is, of itself, enough to fill the wishes of the most aspiring mind, and no doubt the place would be sought as eagerly as it now is, though not a dollar should be given to the man who fills it; but because his station exposes him to great expenses he is allowed a salary sufficient to meet them.

Q207. What is the amount of the President's salary, that is, the sum of money paid him by the United States every year?
A. It is at present fixed at twenty-five thousand dollars.

Q208. May he receive any other money from the United States, or from any one State?
A. No; he is expressly forbidden to receive any other sum of money than his salary.

Q209. Why?
A. Lest, if any State allowed him money, he might be led to favor that State more than the others; and lest, if he was suffered to receive other sums from the United States, he might amass so much money as should make him a dangerous citizen to a free country.

Q210. Does the President take an oath before he enters upon his office?
A. Yes.

Q211. What is an oath?
A. It is a solemn calling upon God, who knows the hearts of all men, and will call every man to account for his conduct in this world, to bear witness that what a man says is true, or that what he promises he means to perform.

Q212. What is the President's oath of office?
A. It is in these words - "I do solemnly swear, that I will faithfully execute the office of President of the United States; and will, to the best of my ability, preserve, protect, and defend the Constitution of the United States."

Q213. What are the powers which belong to the President?

A.   He is commander and chief, both of the army and navy; every officer of both, from the highest to the lowest, is obliged to obey his orders.

Q214.   Are the officers of the militia obliged to obey them?
A.   Yes, whenever the militia are called out in the service of the United States; (at other times they are under the command of the Governors of their own States).

Q215.   Has he any other powers?
A.   Yes; he may grant reprieves and pardons for offences against the United States.

Q216.   What is a reprieve?
A.   When a person has been tried, found guilty, and condemned to be punished on a certain day, a reprieve is a putting off of the punishment to some other time.

Q217.   What is a pardon?
A.   It is a delivering of a condemned person from the punishment of his offence. A reprieve only delays punishment, a pardon prevents it entirely.

Q218.   May the President do this in all cases of offences against the United States?
A.   In all cases, except cases of impeachment.

Q219.   What other powers has he?
A.   He has a very solemn power, that of making Treaties for the United States with other nations.

Q220.   Why is this a solemn power?
A.   Because a treaty is the supreme law of the land, and usually concerns matters of great importance to us all. *

Q221.   Is nobody joined with the President in this power? or may he make any agreement he thinks fit, with other nations?
A.   This power is so great and weighty, that the Constitution will entrust it to no one man. Even the President cannot make a treaty without the consent of the Senate of the United States; nor is it sufficient that a majority of the Senate agree to it; two thirds of all the Senators who are present when the vote is taken, must agree to any treaty, before it is binding on the United States.

Q222.   Has the President any other power?
A.   Yes; powers of nomination and appointment.

Q223.   What do you mean by this?

---

* See Editor's Notes on Pages 48-52 after the Catechism. It is critical that you read all of the notes. You are encouraged to write us with your criticisms and comments and help us to improve this work in a later edition.

A. When persons are to be employed to do the duties of certain great public offices, none can be so employed but those whom the President first nominates; that is, proposes to the Senate, and whom the Senate consent to have employed; and when the Senate have given this consent, the persons cannot act in their office till they receive orders to do so from their President; -such an order is called their appointment, and when put in writing it is called their commission.

Q224. What officers are appointed in this manner?
A. Ambassadors and foreign Ministers; (that is, persons sent by the United States to the Government of some other nation, either to prepare some public treaty, or to reside there as the representative of this country). Consuls, (persons sent by this country to reside in the ports of other nations, to protect our commerce; that is, to see that our vessels, our sailors, and the property of our merchants, are properly treated there, according to the treaties and laws of both countries). Judges of the Supreme Court, and all other officers of the United States, except those who are expressly ordered by the Constitution to be appointed by some other person than the President.

Q225. May the President appoint any officer without the consent of the Senate?
A. Yes, if Congress makes a law giving him the power, but this applies only to inferior officers, that is, such as have other officers over them.

Q226. May Congress give the appointment of such officers to any other than the President?
A. Yes; it may give it to the Courts of Law, or to the Heads of Departments.

Q227. What do you mean by the Heads of Departments?
A. This name is given to certain officers who have the chief care under the President, of the four great branches of the Government, called the Executive Departments; and who are called the Secretary of State, the Secretary of the Treasury, the Secretary of War, and the Secretary of the Navy.

Q228. Are the duties of these officers declared by the Constitution?
A. No; but by law of Congress. They are, however, persons of great importance in our government. The Secretary of State attends to every thing which concerns our affairs with other nations; and also to those of the General Government with the Governments of the different States; the Secretary of the Treasury attends to all that concerns the money of the United States; the Secretary of War manages the business of the army; and the Secretary of the Navy that which concerns the vessels of war. All these officers are, however, under the control of the President; he may require their opinion in writing on any subject that belongs to their different departments, but he is not bound by it; he may also dismiss them from office.

Q229. Suppose any of the officers whom the President has appointed by the consent of the Senate should die, or should resign from office, while the Senate is not sitting; what is to be done?
A. The President may appoint another person in his place who shall hold the office till the end of the next meeting of the Senate.

Q230. What are the duties of the President?
A. He must from time to time give information to Congress of the state of the United States.

Q231. Does he know what is the state of the nation better than the members of Congress?
A. Yes; his office is such that he has a better opportunity of knowing it. Each member of Congress resides only in one State, but the President resides in a spot in the middle of them all. It is the duty of all officers below him, to send reports of the various affairs in which they are employed, to one or other of the Heads of Departments, and these lay all the knowledge they thus obtain, before the President for his direction and assistance in the many and great duties he has to perform. He is, therefore, of all persons, best acquainted with the general concerns of this nation.

Q232. When does he lay this information before Congress?
A. He makes a very full statement of it when they first meet, in what is usually called the President's Speech; and from time to time, while the two Houses are met, he sends to each of them messages, in which he gives more particular statements than he could do in his first general speech.

Q233. Suppose Congress wish to know from the President something which he has not told them in his speech or messages, may they call upon him to communicate it?
A. Yes, and if he does not think that the public good requires it to be kept secret, he always answers the call, and gives them the knowledge they desired, if he can do so.

Q234. Does he do more than communicate information to Congress?
A. Yes; his duty is also to recommend to them such things as he thinks will be for the advantage of the country.

Q235. Are they obliged to do as he advises?
A. No. They pay respectful attention to what he says to them, and listen to the reasons he gives in favor of the measures he recommends, but they are at full liberty to follow their own judgments in all cases.

Q236. Is it desirable that Congress should always comply with the advice of the President?

A. No; for then his advice would, in time, come to have the authority of a command; it would be the President and not Congress who made the laws; and the liberty of the country would be in the greatest danger. There is no more dangerous despot than one who can make his will obeyed, and yet preserve the forms of a free government. August Caesar ruled the whole Roman Empire with absolute sway, yet did every thing by resolves of the Senate, as if Rome was free.

Q237. Suppose some very important matter should happen while Congress is not met, can the President call them together?
A. Yes. He can call either or both Houses, or only one; if any law is to be made, both Houses must be called; if only a treaty or an appointment is to be made, the Senate only need be assembled.

Q238. Suppose, when both Houses are met, they should find themselves unable to agree about the time at which they will adjourn, (that is, cease to meet) can the President end the dispute?
A. Yes, by adjourning both Houses.

Q239. In that case, when are they to meet again?
A. At any time the President fixes, when he adjourns them.

Q240. What other duty is required of the President?
A. He must receive all ambassadors and foreign ministers, that is, persons sent by other nations to make treaties with us, or to reside here as representatives of their own government.

Q241. Has he any other duty?
A. Yes, he has one great, general, and constant duty for which all this power is put at his command, -it is to take care that the laws shall be faithfully executed; that is, that whatever Congress orders shall be done, and whoever disobeys the laws shall be punished.

Q242. May he be punished himself?
A. We have already seen that every civil officer of the United States may be impeached by the House of Representatives, tried before the Senate, and, if guilty, may be turned out of office. The crimes for which this is done are chiefly treason and bribery. Treason, we said, is making war against the United States, by endeavoring to resist or overturn the government; bribery means the unlawful taking of money by any officer for doing or omitting some act of his office.

Q243. Does not every officer receive money for doing the duties of his office?
A. Yes, the law allows him a certain sum; but a bribe is something more than this, given to him not by the United States, but by somebody who wishes him to favor them in the exercise of his power as a public officer. It is wicked to offer a bribe, it is still worse to accept one.

Q244. Can there be no bribery but by means of money?
A. Yes; bribes may be offered in various shapes; any benefit or advantage offered to an officer for an improper end is a bribe.

Q245. What do you understand by a Court?
A. A place where a Judge sits to hear and determine causes according to law.

Q246. Are Courts necessary?
A. Certainly. Wherever laws are made there must be some way of determining when they have been disobeyed, and of causing those who disobey them to be punished. This is the use of a Court and of a Judge. When one person believes that another has broken the laws, to his injury, or to the injury of the public, he may cause that person to appear before a Judge and have it determined by witnesses, whether he has broken the laws or not; and if he has, he is forced to suffer such a punishment as the law directs.

Q247. Are there also Courts in every State of the United States?
A. Yes. Each State appoints Judges of its own to see that its laws are executed.

Q248. Are there also other Courts belonging to no particular State but to the United States?
A. Yes.

Q249. Are all these Courts equal, or is one superior to another?
A. They are not all equal - but in each State some of the State Courts are set over others; and so it is with the Courts of the United States.

Q250. Why are they not all equal?
A. Some are set over others, in order, that if one makes any mistake it may be corrected by that above it. When a citizen thinks he has been wronged in a lower Court, he may take his cause to a higher one; this is called an appeal; and if in this higher Court, he still thinks he is wronged, he may appeal to a court higher still, until he has got to the highest Court in his own State.

Q251. Can he take his cause from the State Courts to the Courts of the United States?
A. No: not unless his cause has to do with a law made by a State, which he supposes is contrary to the Constitution of the United States. That question can be settled only by the Supreme Court of the United States.

Q252. Suppose his cause has to do with a law of the United States and not State law?
A. He must go at once to the Courts of the United States.

Q253. What are these?

A. They consist of one Supreme Court, (the highest of all), and of such other Courts, under this, as Congress may from time to time establish.

Q254. Has Congress established any?
A. Yes - it has appointed some which are called Circuit Courts of the United States; and others, below these, which are called District Courts of the United States.

Q255. What Judges sit in the Circuit Courts of the United States?
A. The Judges of the United States Supreme Court.

Q256. What Judges sit in the District Courts of the United States?
A. District Judges.

Q257. What kind of causes are tried in the Courts of the United States?
A. Any cause must be tried there in which the dispute is about the true meaning of any part of the Constitution.

Q258. What else?
A. All causes under the laws of the United States.

Q259. Any others?
A. Yes; all which depend upon treaties between the United States and other nations.

Q260. What other causes?
A. All in which Ambassadors or other public Ministers, or Consuls, sent to the United States by other governments, are parties concerned.

Q261. What others?
A. All causes which concern the taking or detaining of ships at sea, and all which concern crimes committed at sea, or in harbors, or rivers - or in forts and dockyards, belonging to the United States.

Q262. What other causes are tried in these Courts?
A. All disputes in which the United States is a party; all disputes between one State and another State; all in which one of the States sues any person that is the citizen of another of the States; all in which a citizen of one State sues a citizen of another State; all in which citizens of one and the same State lay claim to land under grants of different States; all in which one of the States sues a citizen of some foreign country; and all in which citizens of the United States, and citizens of any other country sue each other. But not where the citizens of one State sue another State; or where citizens or subjects of a foreign State sue one of the States of the Union.

Q263. Must all causes of these several kinds be begun in one of the inferior courts of the United States, or may any of them be commenced at once in the Supreme Court?

A. All cases which have to do with ambassadors, public ministers, and consuls, and all those in which one of the States is a party, may be begun in the Supreme Court, the others, after being commenced in the inferior Courts of the United States, may be removed to the Supreme Court by an appeal; -but this is submitted to the regulation of Congress, who may determine by law when it may be done, and in what manner.

Q264. How are the Judges of the Courts of the United States appointed?
A. By the President, with the advice and consent of the Senate.

Q265. How long do they remain in office?
A. During good behavior; that is, until they resign their office or are turned out of it for some great offense.

Q266. Why are not Judges elected from time to time, like Members of the House of Representatives and Senators? and why may they not be removed from their offices unless they are proved to be guilty of great offenses?
A. If Judges held their places at the mere good pleasure of the people, they would be greatly tempted to act in a partial and improper manner in order to please those who chose them to office, and to keep their favor; but when they know that no man or number of men can turn them out of office so long as they do their duty, they administer justice without fear and with an equal regard to all who ask it.

Q267. Why then should not Legislators hold their office in the same way?
A. Because they make the laws, while Judges only explain and apply them; it would be very dangerous to liberty to give our law makers power for life; they require restraint lest they should become our tyrants; -therefore their time in office is made short, so that if the people thought them unwise or unfaithful they may refuse to give them the office again. *

Q268. You said that the use of Courts was to determine when the laws have been disobeyed, and causing those who have disobeyed them to be punished. How do courts answer this end?
A. When a person is charged with having done something to his neighbor, or to the State, which is forbidden by law, the fact is judged by a Jury. *

Q269. What do you mean by a Jury?

---

* See Editor's Notes on Pages 48-52 after the Catechism. It is critical that you read all of the notes. You are encouraged to write us with your criticisms and comments and help us to improve this work in a later edition.

A.   A company of citizens, chosen by lot, and who have no interest in the matter, who listen to the proofs brought against the person accused, and who then agree among themselves whether the accusation has been proved or not. When they declare this agreement in opinion, it is called a verdict; and according to this, the cause is decided. *

Q270.   Is this a wise regulation?
A.   Certainly. The trial by jury is a most precious privilege - as it secures to every man a fair hearing, and is the best safe-guard of his liberty, property, and life; all which might be taken from him by a partial or corrupt Judge, if that officer alone had to decide on the guilt or innocence of those who are tried before him.

Q271.   Does a Jury decide in civil suits as well as in criminal prosecutions?
A.   I do not understand the difference between them.

Q272.   By a civil suit, I mean one citizen's calling another into court to answer him for some injury committed against him; by a criminal prosecution, I mean a citizen's being brought up by a public accuser for some crime committed against society at large, and for which he is liable to public punishment.
A.   A jury decides in both cases. When an officer of the United States is impeached, the accuser is the House of Representatives, and the jury is the Senate; but in ordinary prosecutions and suits, the jury consists of twelve persons, residing near the place where the act was committed.

Q273.   May an accused person be tried in a different State from that which the criminal act was committed?
A.   No.

Q274.   Suppose the act was committed at sea, or in some other place not within any of the States of the Union; where must the trial be held?
A.   Where Congress shall have appointed by law.

Q275.   Ought all the public acts of a State, and of all its courts and officers, to be recorded in writing?
A.   Certainly; not only to preserve a remembrance of them, but that those persons who are affected by these acts may be able to show proof of them, and if injured, to obtain redress.

Q276.   When such a record is made in one of the States, and a copy of it, duly proved, is given, must that record be received as proof by all the other States?
A.   Yes. But Congress may determine by law in what manner the record shall be proved for this purpose.

---

* See Editor's Notes on Pages 48-52 after the Catechism. It is critical that you read all of the notes. You are encouraged to write us with your criticisms and comments and help us to improve this work in a later edition.

Q277. When a citizen of one State goes into any other State of the Union, may he be treated as if he was a foreigner? or may any difference be made between his privileges and those of the citizens of that State?
A. No. He shall enjoy every privilege which they do.

Q278. If a person charged with a crime in one State, shall flee from justice into the bounds of another State, is he safe from pursuit and trial?
A. No. If the Governor of the State where the crime was committed applies to the governor of the State where he has taken refuge, the latter shall cause him to be delivered up.

Q279. Suppose a slave in one State shall run away from his master, and flee into another State, does he thereby become free?
A. No. On the application of his master, and proof of his being a slave, he must be given up.

Q280. How many states were there which revolted from Great Britain at the Revolution?
A. Thirteen.

Q281. Did they all agree to the Federal Constitution at the time it went into operation?
A. Not all, but the rest came in soon after.

Q282. Was it then expected that other States would be formed and join the Union?
A. Yes, and provision was made for admitting them.

Q283. By whom were they to be admitted?
A. By Congress.

Q284. Is their number limited?
A. No.

Q285. Or their population?
A. Not by the Constitution; but Congress has determined that a district or territory containing sixty thousand inhabitants may be received into the Union as a State.

Q286. Then that number of people in any State may be erected into a new State?
A. No. No new State can be formed within limits of a State already formed.

Q287. May two states be united by Congress into one? or parts of two States be erected into a third State?
A. Not unless the Legislatures of both such States give their consent.

Q288. When the Colonies separated from Great Britain, was their territory all peopled?

A. No; large tracts of land in several of the States, remained in its natural, wild state.

Q289. When the States united under the Constitution, what was done with these wild lands?
A. They were given up by the several States that owned them, and set apart as common property, for the good of the whole.

Q290. Who has power to govern these territories as they become settled and to sell the land to the settlers?
A. The Congress of the United States.

Q291. Have they since been extensively settled?
A. Yes. Many new States have been formed within their limits, and many more are expected to be. They are in the mean while divided into several distinct portions called territories, each of which has a form of government suited to its amount of population, and a Delegate in Congress with power to speak, but not to vote in that body.

Q292. Has any State the right to set up a monarchical form of government for itself, that is a government where the supreme power is in the hands of a king?
A. No. When the Colonies united they were all republics, the new government they formed for the Union was republican, and they then secured to every State which had joined or should join the confederation, a republican form of government.

Q293. Who is to see that this regulation is carried into effect?
A. The Congress.

Q294. Does Congress secure any other privilege to the different States?
A. Yes. It must protect them from invasion by an enemy. This is one of the most important benefits of our Union; each State has the protection of the whole.

Q295. Should unruly persons in any of the States attempt by violence to resist and overturn the State Government, and should they gain such strength that the State is not able to quell them, must Congress interfere?
A. Yes, if applied to by the Governor or Legislature of such State. But not to prevent a peaceable alteration of the laws attempted in a regular and proper manner.

Q296. The majority of the people of any State may certainly alter its laws, provided they do not violate the Constitution: but may the Constitution itself be altered?
A. Yes. The Constitution being nothing more than an expression of the will of the people of the United States, is at all times within their own power, and they may change it as they like, but it ought not to be changed till it is very clearly shown to be the wish of the people.

Q297. How is this to be found out?
A. When two thirds of the members both of the Senate and the House of Representatives shall agree in opinion that an alteration would be proper, they may state such alteration and propose it to be considered by the people of all the States. The alteration must then be considered by the Legislature of each of the States, or by a Convention in each State, (which is a meeting of persons chosen by the people for this particular purpose); and if three fourths of the States agree to the amendment, it then becomes a part of the Constitution.

Q298. But if three fourths of the States should thus agree to an amendment which would deprive the remaining States against their will of their equal vote in the Senate, would such amendment be binding?
A. No. This case is provided against in the Constitution, and one other (in relation to slaves) which could only happen previous to the year 1808; but as that year is now past, no farther notice need be taken of it.

Q299. What is the supreme law of the United States?
A. The Constitution itself is supreme; and all laws and treaties made by Congress and the President, in conformity with it, are superior to any law made by one of the States, so that if the law of a State contradicts a law of Congress, the State law is of no force, and the United States law alone must be obeyed.

Q300. What security have we that the Constitution will be observed?
A. The President, the Members of Congress, the Members of all the State Legislatures, and all public officers of the United States, and of each one of the States, takes an oath, when they enter upon their several offices, to obey the Constitution. But the great security for its observance lies in the wisdom and excellence of the Constitution itself, and the conviction of the whole people of the United States, that it is for their true interest to observe it inviolate. It has been tried for fifty years, and has done more to render this nation peaceable, powerful, and happy than any form of government that ever existed among men.

Q301. You said that the Constitution, however wise and good, might nevertheless be amended if the people of the United States choose?
A. Yes; the Constitution says so expressly.

Q302. Has it ever been amended?
A. Yes, several times.

Q303. What was the subject of the first amendment?
A. The subject of religious freedom.

Q304. What do you mean by that?

A.   I mean the right every man has to worship God in such way as he thinks fit, without being called to account for his opinions, or punished for them.

Q305.   Is this a sacred right, which ought to be guarded with the greatest care?
A.   Certainly. God alone is the Judge of our religious belief and service, and no man has a right to interfere with it, so long as it does not lead us to injure or disturb our neighbor. A great part of the misery and oppression which has existed in the world, began with forcing men to do what their conscience disapproved.

Q306.   What amendment was made in the Constitution on this subject?
A.   Congress was forbidden to make any law respecting an establishment of religion; that is, giving preference to any one form of religion above another, and making laws to support it; or making laws to prevent men from freely holding or observing any particular form of religious belief and practice.

Q307.   Was any other subject introduced into the same amendment?
A.   Yes; the freedom of speech and the freedom of the press.

Q308.   What do you understand by these expressions?
A.   In a free country like ours, every citizen has a right to express his opinion of the character and conduct of our rulers, and of the laws they make for our government; to forbid this, or punish it, would be highly dangerous to our liberty. If those chosen by their fellow citizens to rule the State, rule in a foolish or wicked manner, it ought to be known, that they may be speedily turned out of office; but if nobody might find fault with them without danger of punishment, their bad conduct would never be exposed, and they might continue in power to the great injury of us all. The right to speak our opinions is the freedom of speech; and the right to print them, is the freedom of the press that they may be read by others. *

Q309.   But suppose I say of my rulers what is false and injurious, may I not be punished?
A.   Yes, if they can prove in a court of justice that what you have said is false, and that your saying or publishing it has injured them. So may any of your fellow citizens. But you are still at liberty to speak and to print, being liable to the consequences if you abuse your liberty.

Q310.   If the people shall be of the opinion that any of the acts of their rulers have been wrong, may they meet together to petition, that is publicly to ask, that these acts may be altered?
A.   Yes, if they meet peaceably; but if they behave in a riotous or disorderly manner, they may, and ought to be punished.

---

* See Editor's Notes on Pages 48-52 after the Catechism. It is critical that you read all of the notes. You are encouraged to write us with your criticisms and comments and help us to improve this work in a later edition.

Q311. May they meet with arms in their hands?
A. Yes; the right to keep and to carry arms is one which belongs to the citizens at all times; but arms must not be used except to support the laws or to resist an enemy.

Q312. As the public safety requires that the Government should employ hired soldiers, as well as the militia, may these soldiers be sent to live in the house of any citizen and at his expense, without his consent?
A. Never, when the nation is at peace. When it is at war, it may often be necessary to do this; but the Constitution declares that even then, it must only be done according to the law; not according to the mere good pleasure of an officer of the army, but in a manner which the Representatives of the people shall lay down.

Q313. Has the Government power to enter the house of a citizen and search it, and to take him, his papers, and his property, at any time it thinks fit?
A. No. It is sometimes necessary and proper to seize a man's person and property, and to search his papers; but this may never be done, until some of his fellow citizens charge him with some offence which would require this to be done, make it appear probable that he is guilty, and swear to what they declare against him. Then a Judge gives to an officer a warrant to search or to seize; but the warrant must say particularly what places are to be searched, and what persons or property is to be seized. Otherwise no man would be secure.

Q314. Suppose I am accused by my neighbor of some crime which is punished with death, (these are called capital crimes) or which would render me infamous in society; must I be seized and tried because he has accused me?
A. No. You must be either confined or in some other manner prevented from going away, until his accusation is laid before a number of your fellow citizens, called a Grand Jury, who swear to act fairly in the case. They hear your accuser and all the proof he has to bring against you, and if they think that he is wrong in supposing you guilty, and that his proof is not sufficient, they refuse to have you tried, and you are set at liberty. But if they think his proof is such that you ought to be tried, they deliver to the Court what is called a Bill of Indictment; that is, a paper setting forth the crime you are said to have done, and according to this you are tried. So that no man can be put on his trial, till many impartial men think and swear that there is reason to believe he is guilty.

Q315. Does what you have now said, apply to soldiers and sailors in the army and the fleet?
A. No; they are tried according to certain rules and regulations, called articles of war, to which they swear to submit when they become soldiers or sailors.

Q316. Does it apply to citizens who are in the militia?

A. No, not when engaged in actual service, in time of war or public danger; they are then subjects to the articles of war. It applies to them at all other times.

Q317. What other rights are secured to an accused person?
A. Whoever is accused of a criminal offence, (that means an offence for which he is to be tried by the State) shall have a speedy and public trial. He may not be kept confined longer than is necessary, nor may he be tried in a secret place, but openly before all who choose to attend. And he shall have a Jury of impartial men to try him. (The trial by Jury has already been explained.) The men who compose his jury must be of the same State, and of the same district, where the offense is said to have been committed. He must be fully informed of the nature of the charge brought against him, and how it came to be made.

Q318. Suppose he knows of persons who could prove him not guilty of the charge, but they live far off, or are unwilling to attend his trial, can he force them to come?
A. Yes. The Court will grant him a certain paper, called a Writ of Subpoena, and send it by an officer, to every person he wants as a witness in his favor; and such persons are obliged to come, or be heavily punished.

Q319. Has he any other privilege?
A. Yes, he has the right to have the advice of a lawyer to aid him in his defence, and to plead his cause.

Q320. Can he be forced to bear witness against himself?
A. No.

Q321. If he is once tried and not found guilty, may he be again tried for the same offence?
A. If it is an offence, which if proved against him, would put him in danger of losing life, or suffering any bodily injury, he may not.

Q322. Are my life, liberty, and property guarded by the Constitution, so that no man is allowed to touch either of them, except according to the laws of the land?
A. They are.

Q323. But if my property is wanted for a useful public object, may it not be taken from me?
A. Yes, but you must be paid the full value of it in money.

Q324. Suppose I am sued by my neighbor, about some property, am I to have a Jury to try the cause?
A. Yes, if the amount in dispute is more than twenty dollars.

Q325. You said that when a person is charged with a criminal offence, he must be confined, or otherwise prevented from going away, till a Grand Jury has heard the accusation and proof against him. How else can he be restrained from going off, but by confining him?

A. By obliging him to bring forward persons who will become his Bail; that means, who will agree to forfeit a certain sum of money if he goes away and does not return to be tried.

Q326. Who has the power to say how much money they shall agree to forfeit?
A. The Judge, before whom the man is accused.

Q327. May he fix any sum he pleases?
A. No. The sum is to be according to the nature of the crime, and the danger of the accused man's running away, but it may not be made so great as to be cruel or unjust.

Q328. Are offences ever punished by a fine; that is, by obliging the offender to pay a sum of money?
A. Yes. But here the same rule applies. The sum must not be made out of proportion to the offence, and the circumstances of the offender.

Q329. May a Judge contrive new punishments out of his own head, or order such as are not in common use for such offence as has been committed?
A. No.

Q330. Because the Constitution only speaks of certain rights belonging to citizens of the United States, does it follow that the citizens have no rights but these?
A. By no means.

Q331. Has the United States Government any power but such as is contained in the Constitution?
A. No.

Q332. Have the different States of the union all the powers which rightfully belong to a State, except those which are denied to them by the Constitution?
A. Yes. When the States united to form a constitution for their General Government, they agreed to give up to that government some of the powers they had before, and they set down in the Constitution what these powers were. All other powers they keep. The same thing is true respecting the people. All the powers they have not given up to the State Governments or to the General Government, they keep in their own hands.

CONCLUSION to the Original 1828 Stansbury Edition

And now, my young friends, having gone through a short, and I hope, clear and intelligible view of this Constitution, I have a few parting words to say to each one of you.

In the first place, consider how happy and how highly favored is our country, in having a system of government so wisely calculated to secure the life, liberty, and happiness of all its citizens. Had you lived or travelled in other parts of the world, you would be much more sensible of this, than you can possibly be without such an opportunity of comparing our lot with that of others. But, as your reading increases, particularly in history and in travels, you will be able to form a more just estimate of what you enjoy. When you read of the oppression which has been, and still is exercised, I do not say in Africa and Asia, whose inhabitants are but partially civilized-- but even in the most enlightened countries of Europe; under absolute monarchs, a proud and haughty nobility ---a worldly, selfish, and ambitious priesthood ---a vast and rapacious standing army, and a host of greedy officers of government; and then turn your eyes on your own happy home, a land where none of these evils has any place ---where the people first make the laws and then obey them ---where they can be oppressed by none, but where every man's person, property, and privileges are surrounded by the law, and sacred from every thing but justice and the public good; how can you be sufficiently grateful to a beneficient Providence, which has thus endowed our country with blessings equally rich and rare?

In the next place, remember that this precious Constitution, thus wise, thus just, is your birth-right. It has been earned for you by your fathers, who counselled much, labored long, and shed their dearest blood, to win it for their children. To them, it was the fruit of toil and danger ---to you, it is a gift. Do not slight it on that account, but prize it as you ought. It is yours, no human power can deprive you of it but your own folly and wickedness. To undervalue, is one of the surest ways to lose it. Take pains to know what the Constitution is ---the more you study, the higher you will esteem it. The better you understand your own rights, the more likely you will be to preserve and guard them.

And, in the last place, my beloved young countrymen, your country's hope, her treasure, and one day to be her pride and her defence; remember that a constitution which gives to the people so much freedom, and entrusts them with so much power, rests for its permanency, on their knowledge and virtue. If you would be free ---if you would see your country grow in all that constitutes true greatness ---cultivate knowledge ---flee from vice. The virtuous citizen is the true noble. He who enlightens his understanding ---controls his passions ---feels for his country's honor ---rejoices in her prosperity ---steps forth to aid her in the hour of danger ---devotes to her advancement the fruits of his mind, and consecrates to her cause, his time, his property, and his noblest powers, such a man is one of God's nobility; he needs no riband nor star; his country knows and remembers his name; nor could any title add to its honor or to his reward. We have seen such men among us; we hope to see many more. And though the glory of giving to their country such a Constitution as this, is what none but they have been so blessed as to enjoy, yet you succeed to a task, but one degree removed from it, that of preserving what they have committed to your virtue, unsullied and unimpaired.

EDITOR'S NOTES

Q36.   The name of the court should be rendered, "supreme Court", with a lower case "s". This is consistently rendered so in the Constitution, that is, lower case "s" for supreme and capital "C" for Court. The intent of law is to be established by the legislature and, in accordance with this, it has been maintained that *case-law is only binding upon the litigants*. The supreme Courts of recent years have usurped in some instances, the powers reserved by the Constitution to the other branches and sit as a continuing, de facto Constitutional Convention in their *interpretation* of laws, in <u>violation</u> of the <u>separation</u> of <u>powers</u> and Article V provisions for Amendment, when it should be applying laws to cases according to **ORIGINAL INTENT.** See EXODUS 18:13 - 26 King James Version.

Q53.   "We hold these truths to be self evident, that all men are created equal... " The Constitution does not call anyone 3/5 of a man as has been alleged by some historical revisionists. But there is a greater question to be settled:

Did the War Between the States truly abolish SLAVERY in the U.S. or was it merely *refined* to include practically all citizens of every race?

Consider the text of the **<u>Hazard Circular</u>** allegedly circulated to bankers in 1862:

"Slavery is likely to be abolished by the war power and chattel slavery destroyed. This, I and my European friends are in favor of, for slavery is but the owning of labor and carries with it the care and feeding of the laborers, while the European plan, led by England, is that capital shall control labor by controlling the money. The great debt that capitalists will see to it is made out of the war, must be used as a means to control the volume of money. To accomplish this the bonds must be used as a banking basis. We are waiting for the Secretary of the Treasury to make this recommendation to Congress."

Any definition of "**SLAVERY**" that does not include a comprehensive understanding of the nature of, and cause and effect relationships between **MONEY, BANKING** and **TAXATION** will prove inadequate to explain the situation that exists in "The Land of the Free and the Home of the Brave" at the end of the twentieth century.

Q99.   One evidence of approaching tyranny is a drastic increase in the volume and complexity of laws, requiring "professional" help for understanding and application. This increased volume and complexity also prevents legislators from either understanding all that is proposed or worse yet, it provides them with an excuse not to know or be accountable for that which is injurious to the people or destructive to Republican government or State sovereignty. Not to mention the *remote* possibility that selfish or evil intent can be concealed.

Q103.   See **Article I: Section 2, Clause 3; Section 8, Clause 1; and Section 9, Clause 4**. These provisions have *never* been *altered, amended* or *repealed*. All *indirect* taxes, ("duties, imposts and excises"), are subject to the rule of *uniformity,* and all *direct* taxes are subject to the rule of *apportionment*. *Direct* taxes must be *apportioned*, and *billed* to the *States*. In addition, the supreme Court has stated that the 16th Amendment "conferred no new power of taxation." See *Stanton v. Baltic Mining Co., 240 US, 112.*, or you may write us for more information on this *compelling* subject.

Q109. Notice that Stansbury answers within the limitations of the **ORIGINAL INTENT** of the "common defense and general welfare" clause. Taxes and duties have proper subjects and objects. That is, taxes are to be imposed *only within the limits of properly delegated authority, only upon proper subjects and only to the extent of Constitutionally limited objectives.*

Q111. **Jefferson** said he would disarm the government of one more power and that was the power to borrow money. **WAS HE PROPHESYING?**

Q116. See **Article I, Section 10, Clause 1. COINING NEVER MEANS PRINTING!** Paper money was strictly prohibited! (See excerpt from Madison's notes pp. 63-64) In addition, the Constitution still prohibits any State from making "any Thing but gold and silver Coin a Tender in Payment of Debts."

Q146. Congress was never vested with any power to "create" money. In a literal sense that means that congress has a responsibility to ensure the monetary system and guard against **counterfeiting** or losses by the people that occur when **currency** is **debased,** (passed at higher than its intrinsic value), or replaced by paper "notes", which were redeemed in gold and silver for various periods of time until eventually redemption was terminated and a fiat "floating" currency was established with no *real* money backing. FIAT means it's only money because the government says it is. Additionally. the **FEDERAL RESERVE BANK (A PRIVATE CORPORATION),** has been used to usurp the proper monetary authority of Congress for the benefit of the stockholders of that corporation. In other words, the national debt, as well as the interest on it, is fraudulent. If you find these facts alarming or confusing, write for more information.

Q154. Read the **Declaration of Independence** carefully, again and again, until you understand it completely. If you do not understand a word, look it up in the **1828 Noah Webster's Dictionary** (Write us for ordering information). In Q154 and its answer, Stansbury seems to confuse a "**privilege**" with a "**right**." These are distinctly different terms. "**Certain Unalienable Rights**" can be given or taken away only by "**their Creator**". The word "privilege" implies a grant from government. Stansbury's equating of rights and privileges may be totally innocent considering the time in which he lived (See his conclusion on page 47). However, in the "light" of the present political situation in these United States this confusion might be tragic.

Q157. See note for Q103 & Q109.

Q170. Stansbury's answer could not be correct in the light of Madison's notes on paper money. On page 557 of *The Formation of the Union,* Madison records that, "Mr.

Elseworth thought this a favorable time to shut and bar the door against paper money." This is clear proof that *that* is exactly what they meant to do. This is further certified by **Article I, Section 10, Clause 1,** prohibiting *anything* but GOLD and SILVER to pass as a tender in the States.

Q180. Study the **Ninth** and **Tenth Amendments** until you understand the principle of **DELEGATION**. Stansbury's words, "ruling over them all" are reminiscent of the **"Divine Right of Kings"**, a concept used in the **"Old World"** to dominate ignorant serfs, but wholly unsuitable for a **FREE PEOPLE**. In the words of the Tenth Amendment: **"The powers not delegated to the United States by the Constitution, nor prohibited by it to the States, are RESERVED to the States respectively and to the PEOPLE."** The Constitution begins *and* ends with **"WE THE PEOPLE"**. God created us for Himself and we created Government for ourselves. A careful reading of the **Declaration of Independence** will make this philosophy of government abundantly clear to any serious reader.

Q220. The language of the Constitution cannot be contorted here to mean that treaties could somehow supersede the Constitution. Otherwise the President's oath would be meaningless. How can a President swear before God to protect and defend the Constitution and then agree to treaties that could *appear* to undermine its authority?

In the Federalist #33, **Alexander Hamilton** discussed this as follows:

"Hence we perceive that the clause which declares the supremacy of the laws of the Union,... only declares a truth, which flows immediately and necessarily from the institution of a federal government. It will not, I presume, have escaped observation, that it expressly confines this supremacy to laws made pursuant to the constitution; which I mention merely as an instance of caution in the convention; since that limitation would have been to be understood, though it had not been expressed."

James Madison, speaking in the framing convention, stated:

"Does it follow, because this power is given to Congress, that it is absolute and unlimited? I do not conceive that power is given to the President and Senate to dismember the empire, or to alienate any great, essential right. I do not think the whole legislative authority have this power. **THE EXERCISE OF THE POWER MUST BE CONSISTENT WITH THE OBJECT OF THE DELEGATION...** The *object of treaties* is the regulation of intercourse with *foreign* nations and is *external*."

In 1801 **Thomas Jefferson** stated in *A Manual on Parliamentary Practice*:

"Treaties are legislative acts. A treaty is a law of the land. It differs from other laws as it must have the consent of a foreign nation, being but a contract with respect to that nation....2. By the general power to make treaties, the Constitution must have intended to comprehend only the objects which are usually regulated by treaty, and cannot be otherwise regulated....3. *It must have meant to except out of these the rights reserved to the States;* for surely the President and Senate cannot do by treaty what the whole Government is interdicted from doing in any way."

Q267. "**THE INTENT OF THE LAW IS THE FORCE OF THE LAW.**" Laws are to be written in **CLEAR LANGUAGE**. A law that cannot be understood by the common man is said to be "**VOID FOR VAGUENESS**". Because, "ignorantia legis non excusat"(ignorance of the law is no excuse). Judges that insist on *EXPLAINING* laws in ways that depart from **ORIGINAL INTENT** are practicing *SOPHISTRY!* According to **NOAH WEBSTER'S 1828 DICTIONARY**, this is "Fallacious reasoning; reasoning sound *in appearance only*." There can be no separation of powers if judges "legislate" from the bench, usurping the authorities granted *only* to the Congress by the Constitution.

Q268. and 269. The **JURY** is to be **JUDGE** of **BOTH** the **LAW** and the **FACTS**. This is a well established principle in American jurisprudence (Write us for ordering information for the Citizen's Rule Book which explains this principle in great detail). Additionally, Stansbury's words "who have no interest in the matter" might be more clearly stated as "who have no *vested* interest". The Jury must always understand their responsibility before God to render Righteous judgment and to stand as a bulwark against tyranny. See Q. & A. 211, regarding an oath.

Q308. Citizens are not "chosen to rule the State". I presume Stansbury is speaking of the United States and I believe a better term might be either "the Union" or the United States. The use of the word "State" with an upper case "S" is foreboding here since, if there was anything the framers wished to avoid it was the consolidation of jurisdictions and breaking down of the separation of powers. Secondly, *public servants* are to be the *obedient subjects* of the **Constitution**--*obeying* it, *promoting* it, and *preserving* the *limitations* and *separation* of *powers*. The Founders and Framers envisioned **NO ALL-POWERFUL, SOCIALIST/MARXIST SUPER-STATE!!!**

Consider the following excerpts:

WASHINGTON'S FAREWELL ADDRESS
United States, September 19, 1796

"Friends, and Fellow-Citizens: The period for a new election of a Citizen, to Administer the Executive government of the United States, being not far distant, and the time actually arrived, when your thoughts must be employed in designating the person, who is to be *clothed* with that important *trust*, it appears to me proper, especially as it may conduce to a more distinct expression of the public voice, that I should now apprise you of the resolution I have formed, to decline being considered among the number of those, out of whom a choice is to be made."

DOCTOR BENJAMIN FRANKLIN
from The Formation of the Union of The United States

"It seems to have been imagined by some that the returning to the mass of the people was degrading the magistrate." [This he thought was contrary to republican principles. (Madison's note)] "In *free* Governments the *rulers* are the *servants*, and the *people* their *superiors* and *sovereigns*. For the former therefore to return among the latter was <u>not</u> to *degrade* but to *promote* them. And it would be imposing an unreasonable burden on them, to keep them always in a **State of servitude**, and not allow them to become again one of the **Masters**."

APPENDIX

The following resource materials can provide the reader with a constructive beginning for further researches into the vital issues that face the United States and its citizens. Even the most casual reader will realize that there has been a **great disparity** between the Constitution and the actions of **our servants** in Washington for the last eighty-five or more years. Remember this advice:

"If ye know these things, happy are ye if ye do them" -John 13:17

I have included a photocopy of the table of contents of *The Formation of the Union of the United States,* as an aid to further studies.

Pages 56-89 [Numbers added for inclusion in this text are at the bottom center of the pages] are excerpted from the above text and pages 90-92 contain the Amendments ratified since the publication of the above text.

According to the American historian, Hamilton Abert Long, there was a meeting that took place where Madison and Jefferson recommended to the Board of Visitors of the University of Virginia, a resolution prescribing the primary source materials which should be used so that all students would be *inculcated* with the basic American governmental principles and that "none should be inculcated which are incompatible with those on which the Constitution of this State, and of the U.S. were genuinely based, in the common opinion." In this meeting six sources were cited that would contain the foundational principles "legitimately developed... " The following list is provided for your further research:

1) ***The Declaration of Independence*** [See pages 58-62, *this text*]

2) ***Washington's Farewell Address***

3) ***The Virginia Resolutions of 1798 & 1799*** [See pages 93,94, *this text*]

4) ***The Federalist*** [Available in most large bookstores]

5) ***Essay Concerning the True and Original Extent of Civil Government***
   --John Locke -1690

6) ***Discourses Concerning Civil Government*** --Algernon Sydney -1698

HOUSE CONCURRENT RESOLUTION NO. 23

[Submitted by Mr. Bacon]

Resolved by the Senate (the House of Representatives concurring), That there shall be compiled, printed with illustrations and bound as may be directed by the Joint Committee on Printing, ten thousand copies of the Madison Debates of the Federal Convention, together with the Declaration of Independence, the Articles of Confederation, the Constitution, the instructions to the Delegates to the Federal Convention, the instruments of ratification of the States, and the texts of the amendments to the Constitution, and other relevant and pertinent historical documents for distribution in the year 1926 in commemoration of the one hundred and fiftieth anniversary of the Declaration of Independence of the United States of America, to the end "that government of the people, by the people, for the people shall not perish from the earth," of which three thousand copies shall be for the use of the Senate and seven thousand copies for the use of the House of Representatives.

Adopted, May 10, 1926.

SELECTED, ARRANGED, AND INDEXED
BY
CHARLES C. TANSILL

PREPARED UNDER THE GENERAL SUPERVISION OF
H. H. B. MEYER
Director, Legislative Reference Service
Library of Congress

THIS VOLUME MAY BE PURCHASED FROM
THE SUPERINTENDENT OF DOCUMENTS
GOVERNMENT PRINTING OFFICE
AT $2.85 PER COPY

69TH CONGRESS, 1ST SESSION - - HOUSE DOCUMENT No. 398

DOCUMENTS

ILLUSTRATIVE
OF THE

FORMATION OF THE UNION OF THE AMERICAN STATES

GOVERNMENT PRINTING OFFICE
WASHINGTON
1927

CONTENTS

	Page
Declaration and resolves of the First Continental Congress, October 14, 1774..	1-5
Resolves adopted in Charlotte Town, Mecklenburg County, N. C., May 31, 1775.	6-9
Declaration of the causes and necessity of taking up arms, July 6, 1775........	10-17
Resolution of secrecy adopted by the Continental Congress, November 9, 1775..	18
Preamble and resolution of the Virginia Convention, May 15, 1776, instructing the Virginia Delegates in the Continental Congress to "propose to that respectable body to declare the United Colonies free and independent States"..	19-20
Resolution introduced in the Continental Congress by Richard Henry Lee (Virginia) proposing a Declaration of Independence, June 7, 1776...........	21
Declaration of Independence, July 4, 1776.................................	22-26
Articles of Confederation, March 1, 1781..................................	27-37
Resolution of the General Assembly of Virginia, January 21, 1786, proposing a joint meeting of commissioners from the States to consider and recommend a Federal plan for regulating commerce.....................................	38
Proceedings of commissioners to remedy defects of the Federal Government, Annapolis, Md., 1786...	39-43
Report of proceedings in Congress, Wednesday, February 21, 1787............	44-46
Ordinance of 1787, July 13, 1787...	47-54
Credentials of the members of the Federal Convention......................	55-84
List of delegates appointed by the States represented in the Federal Convention.	85-86
Notes of Major William Pierce (Georgia) in the Federal Convention of 1787:	
a. Loose sketches and notes taken in the convention, May, 1787..........	87-95
b. Characters in the convention of the States held at Philadelphia, May, 1787..	96-108
Debates in the Federal Convention of 1787 as reported by James Madison....	109-745
Secret proceedings and debates of the convention assembled at Philadelphia, in the year 1787, for the purpose of forming the Constitution of the United States of America. (From the notes taken by the late Robert Yates, Esq., Chief Justice of New York (Albany, 1821))..	746-843
Notes of Rufus King in the Federal Convention of 1787....................	844-878
Notes of William Paterson in the Federal Convention of 1787...............	879-912
Notes of Alexander Hamilton in the Federal Convention of 1787............	913-922
Papers of Dr. James McHenry on the Federal Convention of 1787............	923-952
Variant texts of the Virginia plan presented by Edmund Randolph to the Federal Convention, May 29, 1787:	
Text A...	953-956
Text B...	957-959
Text C...	960-963
The plan of Charles Pinckney (South Carolina), presented to the Federal Convention, May 29, 1787...	964-966

Contents

	Page
Variant texts of the plan presented by William Paterson (New Jersey), to the Federal Convention, June 15, 1787:	
Text A	967–970
Text B	971–974
Text C	975–978
Variant texts of the plan presented by Alexander Hamilton to the Federal Convention, June 18, 1787:	
Text A	979–980
Text B	981–982
Text C	983–984
Text D	985–986
Text E	987–988
The Constitution of the United States	989–1002
Letter of the president of the Federal Convention, September 17, 1787, to the President of Congress, transmitting the Constitution	1003–1004
Resolution of the Federal Convention submitting the Constitution to Congress, September 17, 1787	1005–1006
Resolution of Congress, September 28, 1787, submitting the Constitution to the several States	1007
Circular letter of the Secretary of Congress, September 28, 1787, transmitting copy of the Constitution to the several governors	1008
Ratification of the Constitution by the several States, arranged in the order of their ratification	1009–1059
Resolution of Congress, July 2, 1788, submitting ratifications of the Constitution to a committee	1060–1061
Resolution of the Congress, September 13, 1788, fixing date for the election of a President, and the organization of the Government under the Constitution	1062
Resolution of the First Congress submitting 12 amendments to the Constitution	1063–1065
The first 10 amendments to the Constitution	1066–1067
Subsequent amendments to the Constitution	1068–1072

THE DECLARATION OF INDEPENDENCE—1776 [1]

In Congress, July 4, 1776

THE UNANIMOUS DECLARATION OF THE THIRTEEN UNITED STATES OF AMERICA

WHEN in the Course of human events, it becomes necessary for one people to dissolve the political bands which have connected them with another, and to assume among the powers of the earth, the separate and equal station to which the Laws of Nature and of Nature's God entitle them, a decent respect to the opinions of mankind requires that they should declare the causes which impel them to the separation.—We hold these truths to be self-evident, that all men are created equal, that they are endowed by their Creator with certain unalienable Rights, that among these are Life, Liberty and the pursuit of Happiness.—That to secure these rights, Governments are instituted among Men, deriving their just powers from the consent of the governed,—That whenever any Form of Government becomes destructive of these ends, it is the Right of the People to alter or to abolish it, and to institute new Government, laying its foundation on such principles and organizing its powers in such form, as to them shall seem most likely to effect their Safety and Happiness. Prudence, indeed, will dictate that Governments long established should not be changed for light and transient causes; and accordingly all experience hath shown, that mankind are more disposed to suffer, while evils are sufferable, than to right themselves by abolishing the forms to which they are accustomed. But when a long train of abuses and usurpations, pursuing invariably the same Object evinces a design to reduce them under absolute Despotism, it is their right, it is their duty, to throw off such Government, and to provide new Guards for their future security.—Such has been the patient sufferance of these Colonies; and such is now the necessity which constrains them to alter their former Systems of Government. The history of the present King of Great Britain

---

[1] Printed from the facsimile of the engrossed copy of the original manuscript in the Library of Congress.

is a history of repeated injuries and usurpations, all having in direct object the establishment of an absolute Tyranny over these States. To prove this, let Facts be submitted to a candid world.—He has refused his Assent to Laws, the most wholesome and necessary for the public good.—He has forbidden his Governors to pass Laws of immediate and pressing importance, unless suspended in their operation till his Assent should be obtained; and when so suspended, he has utterly neglected to attend to them.—He has refused to pass other Laws for the accommodation of large districts of people, unless those people would relinquish the right of Representation in the Legislature, a right inestimable to them and formidable to tyrants only.—He has called together legislative bodies at places unusual, uncomfortable, and distant from the depository of their public Records, for the sole purpose of fatiguing them into compliance with his measures.—He has dissolved Representative Houses repeatedly, for opposing with manly firmness his invasions on the rights of the people.—He has refused for a long time, after such dissolutions, to cause others to be elected; whereby the Legislative powers, incapable of Annihilation, have returned to the People at large for their exercise; the State remaining in the mean time exposed to all the dangers of invasion from without, and convulsions within.—He has endeavoured to prevent the population of these States; for that purpose obstructing the Laws for Naturalization of Foreigners; refusing to pass others to encourage their migration hither, and raising the conditions of new Appropriations of Lands.—He has obstructed the Administration of Justice, by refusing his Assent to Laws for establishing Judiciary powers.—He has made Judges dependent on his Will alone, for the tenure of their offices, and the amount and payment of their salaries.—He has erected a multitude of New Offices, and sent hither swarms of Officers to harrass our people, and eat out their substance.—He has kept among us, in times of peace, Standing Armies, without the Consent of our legislatures.—He has affected to render the Military independent of and superior to the Civil power.—He has combined with others to subject us to a jurisdiction foreign to our constitution, and unacknowledged by our laws; giving his Assent to their Acts of pretended Legislation:—For quartering large bodies of armed troops among us:—For protecting them, by a mock Trial, from punishment for any Murders which they should commit on the Inhabitants of these States:—For cutting off our Trade with all parts of the world:—For imposing Taxes on us without our Consent:—For depriving us in many cases, of the benefits of Trial by Jury:—For transporting us beyond Seas to be tried for pretended offences:—For abolishing the free System of English Laws in a neighbouring Province, establishing therein an Arbitrary government, and enlarging its Boundaries so as to render it at once an example and fit instrument for introducing the same absolute rule into these Colonies:—For taking away our Charters, abolishing our most valuable Laws, and altering fundamentally the Forms of our Governments:—For suspending our own Legislatures, and declaring themselves invested with power to legislate for us in all cases whatsoever.—He has abdicated Government here, by declaring us out of his Protection and waging War against us.—He has plundered our seas, ravaged our Coasts, burnt our towns, and destroyed the lives of our people.—He is at this time transporting large Armies of foreign Mercenaries to compleat the works of death, desolation and tyranny, already begun with circumstances of Cruelty & perfidy scarcely paralleled in the most barbarous ages, and totally unworthy the Head of a civilized nation.—He has constrained our fellow Citizens taken Captive on the high Seas to bear Arms against their Country, to become the executioners of their friends and Brethren, or to fall themselves by their Hands.— He has excited domestic insurrections amongst us, and has endeavoured to bring on the inhabitants of our frontiers, the merciless Indian Savages, whose known rule of warfare, is an undistinguished destruction of all ages, sexes and conditions. In every stage of these Oppressions We have Petitioned for Redress in the most humble terms: Our repeated Petitions have been answered only by repeated injury. A Prince, whose character is thus marked by every act which may define a Tyrant, is unfit to be the ruler of a free people. Nor have We been wanting in attentions to our Brittish brethren. We have warned them from time to time of attempts by their legislature to extend an unwarrantable jurisdiction over us. We have reminded them of the circumstances of our emigration and settlement here. We have appealed to their native justice and magnanimity, and we have conjured them by the ties of our common kindred to disavow these usurpations, which, would inevitably interrupt our connections and correspondence. They too have been deaf to the voice of justice and of consanguinity. We must, therefore, acquiesce in the necessity, which denounces our Separation, and hold them, as we hold the rest of mankind, Enemies in War, in Peace Friends.—

WE, THEREFORE, the REPRESENTATIVES of the UNITED STATES OF AMERICA, in General Congress, Assembled, appealing to the Supreme Judge of the world for the rectitude of our intentions, do, in the Name, and by Authority of the good People of these Colonies, solemnly publish and declare, That these United Colonies are, and of Right ought to be FREE AND INDEPENDENT STATES; that they are Absolved from all Allegiance to the British Crown, and that all political connection between them and the State of Great Britain, is and ought to be totally dissolved; and that as Free and Independent States, they have full Power to levy War, conclude Peace, contract Alliances, establish Commerce, and to do all other Acts and Things which Independent States may of right do.—And for the support of this Declaration, with a firm reliance on the protection of Divine Providence, we mutually pledge to each other our Lives, our Fortunes and our sacred Honor.

JOHN HANCOCK.

New Hampshire
 JOSIAH BARTLETT,
 WM. WHIPPLE,
 MATTHEW THORNTON.

Massachusetts Bay
 SAML. ADAMS,
 JOHN ADAMS,
 ROBT. TREAT PAINE,
 ELBRIDGE GERRY

Rhode Island
 STEP. HOPKINS,
 WILLIAM ELLERY.

Connecticut
 ROGER SHERMAN,
 SAM'EL HUNTINGTON,
 WM. WILLIAMS,
 OLIVER WOLCOTT.

New York
 WM. FLOYD,
 PHIL. LIVINGSTON,
 FRANS. LEWIS,
 LEWIS MORRIS.

New Jersey
 RICHD. STOCKTON,
 JNO. WITHERSPOON,
 FRAS. HOPKINSON,
 JOHN HART,
 ABRA. CLARK.

Pennsylvania
 ROBT. MORRIS,
 BENJAMIN RUSH,
 BENJA. FRANKLIN,
 JOHN MORTON,
 GEO. CLYMER,
 JAS. SMITH,
 GEO. TAYLOR,
 JAMES WILSON,
 GEO. ROSS.

Delaware
 CAESAR RODNEY,
 GEO. READ,
 THO. M'KEAN.

Maryland
 SAMUEL CHASE,
 WM. PACA,
 THOS. STONE,
 CHARLES CARROLL of Carrollton.

Virginia
 GEORGE WYTHE,
 RICHARD HENRY LEE,
 TH. JEFFERSON,
 BENJA. HARRISON,
 THS. NELSON, JR.,
 FRANCIS LIGHTFOOT LEE,
 CARTER BRAXTON.

North Carolina
 WM. HOOPER,
 JOSEPH HEWES,
 JOHN PENN.

South Carolina
 EDWARD RUTLEDGE,
 THOS. HEYWARD, JUNR.,
 THOMAS LYNCH, JUNR.,
 ARTHUR MIDDLETON.

Georgia
 BUTTON GWINNETT,
 LYMAN HALL,
 GEO. WALTON.

NOTE.—Mr. Ferdinand Jefferson, Keeper of the Rolls in the Department of State, at Washington, says: "The names of the signers are spelt above as in the facsimile of the original, but the punctuation of them is not always the same; neither do the names of the States appear in the facsimile of the original. The names of the signers of each State are grouped together in the facsimile of the original, except the name of Matthew Thornton, which follows that of Oliver Wolcott."—*Revised Statutes of the United States*, 2d edition, 1878, p. 6.

Formation of the United States

"To establish post-offices." Mr GERRY moved to add, and post-roads. Mr MERCER 2ded & on question

N. H. no. Mas. ay. Ct no. N. J. no. Pena no. Del. ay. Md ay. Va ay. N. C. no. S. C. ay. Geo. ay.

Mr GOVr MORRIS moved to strike out "and emit bills on the credit of the U. States"—If the United States had credit such bills would be unnecessary: if they had not, unjust & useless.

Mr BUTLER, 2ded the motion.

Mr MADISON, will it not be sufficient to prohibit the making them a *tender?* This will remove the temptation to emit them with unjust views. And promissory notes in that shape may in some emergencies be best.

Mr GOVr MORRIS. striking out the words will leave room still for notes of a *responsible* minister which will do all the good without the mischief. The Monied interest will oppose the plan of Government, if paper emissions be not prohibited.

Mr GHORUM was for striking out, without inserting any prohibition. if the words stand they may suggest and lead to the measure.

Col. MASON had doubts on the subject. Congs he thought would not have the power unless it were expressed. Though he had a mortal hatred to paper money, yet as he could not foresee all emergences, he was unwilling to tie the hands of the Legislature. He observed that the late war could not have been carried on, had such a prohibition existed.

Mr GHORUM. The power as far as it will be necessary or safe, is involved in that of borrowing.

Mr MERCER was a friend to paper money, though in the present state & temper of America, he should neither propose nor approve of such a measure. He was consequently opposed to a prohibition of it altogether. It will stamp suspicion on the Government to deny it a discretion on this point. It was impolitic also to excite the opposition of all those who were friends to paper money. The people of property would be sure to be on the side of the plan, and it was impolitic to purchase their further attachment with the loss of the opposite class of Citizens

---

[54] The words "The clause" are here inserted in the transcript.
[55] The word "the" is here inserted in the transcript.
[56] In the transcript the vote reads: "Massachusetts, Delaware, Maryland, Virginia, South Carolina, Georgia, aye—6; New Hampshire, Connecticut, New Jersey, Pennsylvania, North Carolina, no—5."
[59] The word "Mr." is substituted in the transcript for "Col."

M!̣ Elseworth thought this a favorable moment to shut and bar the door against paper money. The mischiefs of the various experiments which had been made, were now fresh in the public mind and had excited the disgust of all the respectable part of America. By witholding the power from the new Govern! more friends of influence would be gained to it than by almost any thing else. Paper money can in no case be necessary. Give the Government. credit, and other resources will offer. The power may do harm, never good.

M!̣ Randolph, notwithstanding his antipathy to paper money, could not agree to strike out the words, as he could not foresee all the occasions which *⁶⁰* might arise.

M!̣ Wilson. It will have a most salutary influence on the credit of the U. States to remove the possibility of paper money. This expedient can never succeed whilst its mischiefs are remembered, and as long as it can be resorted to, it will be a bar to other resources.

M!̣ Butler. remarked that paper was a legal tender in no Country in Europe. He was urgent for disarming the Government of such a power.

M!̣ Mason was still averse to tying the hands of the Legislature *altogether*. If there was no example in Europe as just remarked, it might be observed on the other side, that there was none in which the Government was restrained on this head.

M!̣ Read, thought the words, if not struck out, would be as alarming as the mark of the Beast in Revelations.

M!̣ Langdon had rather reject the whole plan than retain the three words " (and emit bills ")

On the motion for striking out

N. H. ay. Mas. ay. C!̣ ay. N. J. no. P!̣ ay. Del. ay. M!̣ no. V!̣ ay.* N. C. ay. S. C. ay. Geo. ay.⁶¹

The clause for borrowing money,⁶² agreed to nem. con.

Adj!̣

---

⁶⁰ The word "that" is substituted in the transcript for "which."

⁶¹ In the transcript the vote reads: "New Hampshire, Massachusetts, Connecticut, Pennsylvania, Delaware, Virginia,⁶ North Carolina, South Carolina, Georgia, aye—9; New Jersey, Maryland, no—2."

⁶ This vote in the affirmative [by Virg!̣ was occasioned by the acquiescence of M!̣ Madison who became satisfied that striking out the words would not disable the Gov!̣ from the use of public notes as far as they could be safe & proper; & would only cut off the pretext for a paper currency, ⁶³ and particularly for making the bills a tender ⁶⁴ either for public or private debts.

⁶³ The transcript italicizes the words "paper currency" and "a tender."

⁶⁴ The word "was" is here inserted in the transcript.

general confusion, and an ultimate decision by the sword, he should give the plan his support.

Mr GERRY, stated the objections which determined him to withhold his name from the Constitution. 1. the duration and re-eligibility of the Senate. 2. the power of the House of Representatives to conceal their journals. 3. the power of Congress over the places of election. 4 the unlimited power of Congress over their own compensations. 5.* Massachusetts has not a due share of Representatives allotted to her. 6.* 3/5 of the Blacks are to be represented as if they were freemen. 7.* Under the power over commerce, monopolies may be established. 8. The vice president being made head of the Senate. He could however he said get over all these, if the rights of the Citizens were not rendered insecure 1.[1] by the general power of the Legislature to make what laws they may please to call necessary and proper. 2.[2] raise armies and money without limit. 3.[3] to establish a tribunal without juries, which will be a Star-chamber as to Civil cases. Under such a view of the Constitution, the best that could be done he conceived was to provide for a second general Convention.

On the question on the proposition of Mr Randolph. All the States answered—no

On the question to agree to the Constitution, as amended. All the States ay.

The Constitution was then ordered to be engrossed.

And the House adjourned.

MONDAY SEPR 17. 1787:[4] IN CONVENTION

The engrossed Constitution being read,

Docr FRANKLIN rose with a speech in his hand, which he had reduced to writing for his own conveniency,[5] and which Mr Wilson read in the words following.

---

* The word "that" is here inserted in the transcript.
[1] The figure "1" is changed in the transcript to "first."
[2] The figure "2" is changed in the transcript to "secondly, to."
[3] The figure "3" is changed in the transcript to "thirdly."
[4] The year "1787" is omitted in the transcript.
[5] The word "conveniency" is changed in the transcript to "convenience."

Mr President

I confess that there are several parts of this constitution which I do not at present approve, but I am not sure I shall never approve them: For having lived long, I have experienced many instances of being obliged by better information, or fuller consideration, to change opinions even on important subjects, which I once thought right, but found to be otherwise. It is therefore that the older I grow, the more apt I am to doubt my own judgment, and to pay more respect to the judgment of others. Most men indeed as well as most sects in Religion, think themselves in possession of all truth, and that wherever others differ from them it is so far error. Steele a Protestant in a Dedication tells the Pope, that the only difference between our Churches in their opinions of the certainty of their doctrines is, the Church of Rome is infallible and the Church of England is never in the wrong. But though many private persons think almost as highly of their own infallibility as of that of their sect, few express it so naturally as a certain french lady, who in a dispute with her sister, said "I don't know how it happens, Sister but I meet with no body but myself, that's always in the right—*Il n'y a que moi qui a toujours raison.*"

In these sentiments, Sir, I agree to this Constitution with all its faults, if they are such; because I think a general Government necessary for us, and there is no form of Government but what may be a blessing to the people if well administered, and believe farther that this is likely to be well administered for a course of years, and can only end in Despotism, as other forms have done before it, when the people shall become so corrupted as to need despotic Government, being incapable of any other. I doubt too whether any other Convention we can obtain, may be able to make a better Constitution. For when you assemble a number of men to have the advantage of their joint wisdom, you inevitably assemble with those men, all their prejudices, their passions, their errors of opinion, their local interests, and their selfish views. From such an assembly can a perfect production be expected? It therefore astonishes me, Sir, to find this system approaching so near to perfection as it does; and I think it will astonish our enemies, who are waiting with confidence to hear that our councils are confounded like those of the Builders of Babel; and that our States are on the point of separation, only to meet hereafter for the purpose of cutting one another's throats. Thus I consent, Sir, to this Constitution because I expect no better, and because I am not sure, that it is not the best. The opinions I have had of its errors, I sacrifice to the public good. I have never whispered a syllable of them abroad. Within these walls they were born, and here they shall die. If every one of us in returning to our Constituents were to report the objections he has had to it, and endeavor to gain partizans in support of them, we might prevent its being generally received, and thereby lose all the salutary effects & great advantages resulting naturally in our favor among foreign Nations as well as among ourselves, from our real or apparent unanimity. Much of the strength & efficiency of any Government in procuring and securing happiness to the people, depends, on opinion, on the general opinion of the goodness of the Government, as well as well as of the wisdom and integrity of its Governors. I hope therefore that for our own sakes as a part of the people, and for the sake of posterity, we shall act heartily and unanimously in recommending this Constitution (if approved by Congress & confirmed by the Conventions) wherever our influence may extend, and turn our future thoughts & endeavors to the means of having it well administred.

On the whole, Sir, I can not help expressing a wish that every member of the Convention who may still have objections to it, would with me, on this occasion doubt a little of his own infallibility, and to make manifest our unanimity, put his name to this instrument.—

He then moved that the Constitution be signed by the members and offered the following as a convenient form viz. " Done in Convention by the unanimous consent of *the States* present the 17ᵗʰ of Sepʳ &c—In Witness whereof we have hereunto subscribed our names."

This ambiguous form had been drawn up by Mʳ G. M. in order to gain the dissenting members, and put into the hands of Docʳ Franklin that it might have the better chance of success.

made of them by those who would wish to prevent the adoption of the Constitution.

M! WILSON prefered the second expedient, he had at one time liked the first best; but as false suggestions may be propagated it should not be made impossible to contradict them.

A question was then put on depositing the Journals and other papers of the Convention in the hands of the President, on which,

N. H. ay. M^ts ay. C! ay. N. J. ay. Pen? ay. Del. ay. M?* no. V? ay. N. C. ay. S. C. ay. Geo. ay.[18]

The President having asked what the Convention meant should be done with the Journals &c, whether copies were to be allowed to the members if applied for. It was Resolved nem: con "that he retain the Journal and other papers, subject to the order of the [19] Congress, if ever formed under the Constitution.

The members then proceeded to sign the instrument.[20]

[21] Whilst the last members were signing it [22] Doct! FRANKLIN looking towards the Presidents Chair, at the back of which a rising sun happened to be painted, observed to a few members near him, that Painters had found it difficult to distinguish in their art a rising from a setting sun. I have said he, often and often in the course of the Session, and the vicisitudes of my hopes and fears as to its issue, looked at that behind the President without being able to tell whether it was rising or setting: But now at length I have the happiness to know that it is a rising and not a setting Sun.

[21] The Constitution being signed by all the members except M! Randolph, M! Mason, and M! Gerry who declined giving it the sanction of their names, the Convention dissolved itself by an Adjournment sine die—

[23] The few alterations and corrections made in these debates which are not in my hand writing, were dictated by me and made in my presence by John C. Payne. JAMES MADISON.

---

* This negative of Maryland was occasioned by the language of the instructions to the Deputies of that State, which required them to report to the State, the *proceedings* of the Convention.

[17] Madison's direction concerning his note is omitted in the transcript.

[18] In the transcript the vote reads; "New Hampshire, Massachusetts, Connecticut, New Jersey, Pennsylvania, Delaware, Virginia, North Carolina, South Carolina, Georgia, aye—10; Maryland,* no—1."

* Transfer.[17]

[19] The word "the" is omitted in the transcript.

[20] In place of the word "instrument," the transcript inserts the following words: "Constitution, as finally amended, as follows." The Constitution is then inserted.

[21] These two final paragraphs of Madison's notes are transposed in the transcript to follow the signatures to the Constitution.

[22] The word "it" is omitted in the transcript.

[23] This statement and Madison's signature are omitted in the transcript.

THE CONSTITUTION OF THE UNITED STATES[1]

We the People of the United States, in Order to form a more perfect Union, establish Justice, insure domestic Tranquility, provide for the common defence, promote the general Welfare, and secure the Blessings of Liberty to ourselves and our Posterity, do ordain and establish this Constitution for the United States of America.

Article. I.

Section. 1. All legislative Powers herein granted shall be vested in a Congress of the United States, which shall consist of a Senate and House of Representatives.

Section. 2. The House of Representatives shall be composed of Members chosen every second Year by the People of the several States, and the Electors in each State shall have the Qualifications requisite for Electors of the most numerous Branch of the State Legislature.

No person shall be a Representative who shall not have attained to the Age of twenty five Years, and been seven Years a Citizen of the United States, and who shall not, when elected, be an Inhabitant of that State in which he shall be chosen.

Representatives and direct Taxes shall be apportioned among the several States which may be included within this Union, according to their respective Numbers, which shall be determined by adding to the whole Number of free Persons, including those bound to Service for a Term of Years, and excluding Indians not taxed, three fifths of all other Persons. The actual Enumeration shall be made within three Years after the first Meeting of the Congress of the United States, and within every subsequent Term of ten Years, in such Manner as they shall by Law direct. The Number of Representatives shall not exceed one for every thirty Thousand,

---

[1] This is a literal copy of the engrossed Constitution as signed. It is in four sheets, with an additional sheet containing the resolutions of transmittal. The note indented at the end is in the original precisely as reproduced here.

but each State shall have at Least one Representative; and until such enumeration shall be made, the State of New Hampshire shall be entitled to chuse three, Massachusetts eight, Rhode-Island and Providence Plantations one, Connecticut five, New-York six, New Jersey four, Pennsylvania eight, Delaware one, Maryland six, Virginia ten, North Carolina five, South Carolina five, and Georgia three.

When vacancies happen in the Representation from any State, the Executive Authority thereof shall issue Writs of Election to fill such Vacancies.

The House of Representatives shall chuse their Speaker and other Officers; and shall have the sole Power of Impeachment.

Section. 3. The Senate of the United States shall be composed of two Senators from each State, chosen by the Legislature thereof, for six Years; and each Senator shall have one Vote.

Immediately after they shall be assembled in Consequence of the first Election, they shall be divided as equally as may be into three Classes. The Seats of the Senators of the first Class shall be vacated at the Expiration of the second Year, of the second Class at the Expiration of the fourth Year, and of the third Class at the Expiration of the sixth Year, so that one third may be chosen every second Year; and if Vacancies happen by Resignation, or otherwise, during the Recess of the Legislature of any State, the Executive thereof may make temporary Appointments until the next Meeting of the Legislature, which shall then fill such Vacancies.

No Person shall be a Senator who shall not have attained to the Age of thirty Years, and been nine Years a Citizen of the United States, and who shall not, when elected, be an Inhabitant of that State for which he shall be chosen.

The Vice President of the United States shall be President of the Senate, but shall have no Vote, unless they be equally divided.

The Senate shall chuse their other Officers, and also a President pro tempore, in the Absence of the Vice President, or when he shall exercise the Office of President of the United States.

The Senate shall have the sole Power to try all Impeachments. When sitting for that Purpose, they shall be on Oath or Affirmation.

When the President of the United States [is tried,] the Chief Justice shall preside: And no Person shall be convicted without the Concurrence of two thirds of the Members present.

Judgment in Cases of Impeachment shall not extend further than to removal from Office, and disqualification to hold and enjoy any Office of honor, Trust or Profit under the United States: but the Party convicted shall nevertheless be liable and subject to Indictment, Trial, Judgment and Punishment, according to Law.

Section. 4. The Times, Places and Manner of holding Elections for Senators and Representatives, shall be prescribed in each State by the Legislature thereof; but the Congress may at any time by Law make or alter such Regulations, except as to the Places of chusing Senators.

The Congress shall assemble at least once in every Year, and such Meeting shall be on the first Monday in December, unless they shall by Law appoint a different Day.

Section. 5. Each House shall be the Judge of the Elections, Returns and Qualifications of its own Members, and a Majority of each shall constitute a Quorum to do Business; but a smaller Number may adjourn from day to day, and may be authorized to compel the Attendance of absent Members, in such Manner, and under such Penalties as each House may provide.

Each House may determine the Rules of its Proceedings, punish its Members for disorderly Behaviour, and, with the Concurrence of two thirds, expel a Member.

Each House shall keep a Journal of its Proceedings, and from time to time publish the same, excepting such Parts as may in their Judgment require Secrecy; and the Yeas and Nays of the Members of either House on any question shall, at the Desire of one fifth of those Present, be entered on the Journal.

Neither House, during the Session of Congress, shall, without the Consent of the other, adjourn for more than three days, nor to any other Place than that in which the two Houses shall be sitting.

Section. 6. The Senators and Representatives shall receive a Compensation for their Services, to be ascertained by Law, and paid out of the Treasury of the United States. They shall in all

Cases, except Treason, Felony and Breach of the Peace, be privileged from Arrest during their Attendance at the Session of their respective Houses, and in going to and returning from the same; and for any Speech or Debate in either House, they shall not be questioned in any other Place.

No Senator or Representative shall, during the Time for which he was elected, be appointed to any civil Office under the Authority. of the United States, which shall have been created, or the Emoluments whereof shall have been encreased during such time; and no Person holding any Office under the United States, shall be a Member of either House during his Continuance in Office.

Section. 7. All Bills for raising Revenue shall originate in the House of Representatives; but the Senate may propose or concur with Amendments as on other Bills.

Every Bill which shall have passed the House of Representatives and the Senate, shall, before it become a Law, be presented to the President of the United States; If he approve he shall sign it, but if not he shall return it, with his Objections to that House in which it shall have originated, who shall enter the Objections at large on their Journal, and proceed to reconsider it. If after such Reconsideration two thirds of that House shall agree to pass the Bill, it shall be sent, together with the Objections, to the other House, by which it shall likewise be reconsidered, and if approved by two thirds of that House, it shall become a Law. But in all such Cases the Votes of both Houses shall be determined by yeas and Nays, and the Names of the Persons voting for and against the Bill shall be entered on the Journal of each House respectively. If any Bill shall not be returned by the President within ten days (Sundays excepted) after it shall have been presented to him, the Same shall be a Law, in like Manner as if he had signed it, unless the Congress by their Adjournment prevent its Return in which Case it shall not be a Law.

Every Order, Resolution, or Vote to which the Concurrence of the Senate and House of Representatives may be necessary (except on a question of Adjournment) shall be presented to the President of the United States; and before the Same shall take Effect, shall be approved by him, or being disapproved by him, shall be repassed by two thirds of the Senate and House of Representatives, according to the Rules and Limitations prescribed in the Case of a Bill.

Section. 8. The Congress shall have Power To lay and collect Taxes, Duties, Imposts and Excises, to pay the Debts and provide for the common Defence and general Welfare of the United States; but all Duties, Imposts and Excises shall be uniform throughout the United States;

To borrow Money on the credit of the United States;

To regulate Commerce with foreign Nations, and among the several States, and with the Indian Tribes;

To establish an uniform Rule of Naturalization, and uniform Laws on the subject of Bankruptcies throughout the United States;

To coin Money, regulate the Value thereof, and of foreign Coin, and fix the Standard of Weights and Measures;

To provide for the Punishment of counterfeiting the Securities and current Coin of the United States;

To establish Post Offices and post Roads;

To promote the Progress of Science and useful Arts, by securing for limited Times to Authors and Inventors the exclusive Right to their respective Writings and Discoveries;

To constitute Tribunals inferior to the supreme Court;

To define and punish Piracies and Felonies committed on the high Seas, and Offences against the Law of Nations;

To declare War, grant Letters of Marque and Reprisal, and make Rules concerning Captures on Land and Water;

To raise and support Armies, but no Appropriation of Money to that Use shall be for a longer Term than two Years;

To provide and maintain a Navy;

To make Rules for the Government and Regulation of the land and naval Forces;

To provide for calling forth the Militia to execute the Laws of the Union, suppress Insurrections and repel Invasions;

To provide for organizing, arming, and disciplining, the Militia, and for governing such Part of them as may be employed in the Service of the United States, reserving to the States respectively, the Appointment of the Officers, and the Authority of training the Militia according to the discipline prescribed by Congress;

To exercise exclusive Legislation in all Cases whatsoever, over such District (not exceeding ten Miles square) as may, by Cession of particular States, and the Acceptance of Congress, become the Seat of the Government of the United States, and to exercise like Authority over all Places purchased by the Consent of the Legislature of the State in which the Same shall be, for the Erection of Forts, Magazines, Arsenals, dock-Yards, and other needful Buildings;—And

To make all Laws which shall be necessary and proper for carrying into Execution the foregoing Powers, and all other Powers vested by this Constitution in the Government of the United States, or in any Department or Officer thereof.

Section. 9. The Migration or Importation of such Persons as any of the States now existing shall think proper to admit, shall not be prohibited by the Congress prior to the Year one thousand eight hundred and eight, but a Tax or duty may be imposed on such Importation, not exceeding ten dollars for each Person.

The Privilege of the Writ of Habeas Corpus shall not be suspended, unless when in Cases of Rebellion or Invasion the public Safety may require it.

No Bill of Attainder or ex post facto Law shall be passed.

No Capitation, or other direct, Tax shall be laid, unless in Proportion to the Census or Enumeration herein before directed to be taken.

No Tax or Duty shall be laid on Articles exported from any State.

No Preference shall be given by any Regulation of Commerce or Revenue to the Ports of one State over those of another: nor shall Vessels bound to, or from, one State, be obliged to enter, clear, or pay Duties in another.

No Money shall be drawn from the Treasury, but in Consequence of Appropriations made by Law; and a regular Statement and Account of the Receipts and Expenditures of all public Money shall be published from time to time.

No Title of Nobility shall be granted by the United States: And no Person holding any Office of Profit or Trust under them, shall, without the Consent of the Congress, accept of any present, Emolument, Office, or Title, of any kind whatever, from any King, Prince, or foreign State.

Section. 10. No State shall enter into any Treaty, Alliance, or Confederation; grant Letters of Marque and Reprisal; coin Money; emit Bills of Credit; make any Thing but gold and silver Coin a Tender in Payment of Debts; pass any Bill of Attainder, ex post facto Law, or Law impairing the Obligation of Contracts, or grant any Title of Nobility.

No State shall, without the Consent of the Congress, lay any Imposts or Duties on Imports or Exports, except what may be absolutely necessary for executing it's inspection Laws: and the net Produce of all Duties and Imposts, laid by any State on Imports or Exports, shall be for the Use of the Treasury of the United States; and all such Laws shall be subject to the Revision and Controul of the Congress.

No State shall, without the Consent of Congress, lay any Duty of Tonnage, keep Troops, or Ships of War in time of Peace, enter into any Agreement or Compact with another State, or with a foreign Power, or engage in War, unless actually invaded, or in such imminent Danger as will not admit of delay.

Article. II.

Section. 1. The executive Power shall be vested in a President of the United States of America. He shall hold his Office during the Term of four Years, and, together with the Vice President, chosen for the same Term, be elected as follows

Each State shall appoint, in such Manner as the Legislature thereof may direct, a Number of Electors, equal to the whole Number of Senators and Representatives to which the State may be entitled in the Congress: but no Senator or Representative, or Person holding an Office of Trust or Profit under the United States, shall be appointed an Elector.

The Electors shall meet in their respective States, and vote by Ballot for two Persons, of whom one at least shall not be an

Inhabitant of the same State with themselves. And they shall make a List of all the Persons voted for, and of the Number of Votes for each; which List they shall sign and certify, and transmit sealed to the Seat of the Government of the United States, directed to the President of the Senate. The President of the Senate shall, in the Presence of the Senate and House of Representatives, open all the Certificates, and the Votes shall then be counted. The Person having the greatest Number of Votes shall be the President, if such Number be a Majority of the whole Number of Electors appointed; and if there be more than one who have such Majority, and have an equal Number of Votes, then the House of Representatives shall immediately chuse by Ballot one of them for President; and if no Person have a Majority, then from the five highest on the List the said House shall in like Manner chuse the President. But in chusing the President, the Votes shall be taken by States, the Representation from each State having one Vote; A quorum for this Purpose shall consist of a Member or Members from two thirds of the States, and a Majority of all the States shall be necessary to a Choice. In every Case, after the Choice of the President, the Person having the greatest Number of Votes of the Electors shall be the Vice President. But if there should remain two or more who have equal Votes, the Senate shall chuse from them by Ballot the Vice President.

The Congress may determine the Time of chusing the Electors, and the Day on which they shall give their Votes; which Day shall be the same throughout the United States.

No Person except a natural born Citizen, or a Citizen of the United States, at the time of the Adoption of this Constitution, shall be eligible to the Office of President; neither shall any Person be eligible to that Office who shall not have attained to the Age of thirty five Years, and been fourteen Years a Resident within the United States.

In Case of the Removal of the President from Office, or of his Death, Resignation, or Inability to discharge the Powers and Duties of the said Office, the Same shall devolve on the Vice President, and the Congress may by Law provide for the Case of

Removal, Death, Resignation or Inability, both of the President and Vice President, declaring what Officer shall then act as President, and such Officer shall act accordingly, until the Disability be removed, or a President shall be elected.

The President shall, at stated Times, receive for his Services, a Compensation, which shall neither be encreased nor diminished during the Period for which he shall have been elected, and he shall not receive within that Period any other Emolument from the United States, or any of them.

Before he enter on the Execution of his Office, he shall take the following Oath or Affirmation:—"I do solemnly swear (or affirm) that I will faithfully execute the Office of President of the United States, and will to the best of my Ability, preserve, protect and defend the Constitution of the United States."

Section. 2. The President shall be Commander in Chief of the Army and Navy of the United States, and of the Militia of the several States, when called into the actual Service of the United States; he may require the Opinion, in writing, of the principal Officer in each of the executive Departments, upon any Subject relating to the Duties of their respective Offices, and he shall have Power to grant Reprieves and Pardons for Offences against the United States, except in Cases of Impeachment.

He shall have Power, by and with the Advice and Consent of the Senate, to make Treaties, provided two thirds of the Senators present concur; and he shall nominate, and by and with the Advice and Consent of the Senate, shall appoint Ambassadors, other public Ministers and Consuls, Judges of the supreme Court, and all other Officers of the United States, whose Appointments are not herein otherwise provided for, and which shall be established by Law: but the Congress may by Law vest the Appointment of such inferior Officers, as they think proper, in the President alone, in the Courts of Law, or in the Heads of Departments.

The President shall have Power to fill up all Vacancies that may happen during the Recess of the Senate, by granting Commissions which shall expire at the End of their next Session.

Section. 3. He shall from time to time give to the Congress Information of the State of the Union, and recommend to their Consideration such Measures as he shall judge necessary and expedient; he may, on extraordinary Occasions, convene both Houses, or either of them, and in Case of Disagreement between them, with Respect to the Time of Adjournment, he may adjourn them to such Time as he shall think proper; he shall receive Ambassadors and other public Ministers; he shall take Care that the Laws be faithfully executed, and shall Commission all the Officers of the United States.

Section. 4. The President, Vice President and all civil Officers of the United States, shall be removed from Office on Impeachment for, and Conviction of, Treason, Bribery, or other high Crimes and Misdemeanors.

Article III.

Section. 1. The judicial Power of the United States, shall be vested in one supreme Court, and in such inferior Courts as the Congress may from time to time ordain and establish. The Judges, both of the supreme and inferior Courts, shall hold their Offices during good Behaviour, and shall, at stated Times, receive for their Services, a Compensation, which shall not be diminished during their Continuance in Office.

Section. 2. The judicial Power shall extend to all Cases, in Law and Equity, arising under this Constitution, the Laws of the United States, and Treaties made, or which shall be made, under their Authority;—to all Cases affecting Ambassadors, other public Ministers and Consuls;—to all Cases of admiralty and maritime Jurisdiction;—to Controversies to which the United States shall be a Party;—to Controversies between two or more States;—between a State and Citizens of another State;—between Citizens of different States,—between Citizens of the same State claiming Lands under Grants of different States, and between a State, or the Citizens thereof, and foreign States, Citizens or Subjects.

In all Cases affecting Ambassadors, other public Ministers and Consuls, and those in which a State shall be Party, the supreme Court shall have original Jurisdiction. In all the other Cases before mentioned, the supreme Court shall have appellate Jurisdiction, both as to Law and Fact, with such Exceptions, and under such Regulations as the Congress shall make.

The Trial of all Crimes, except in Cases of Impeachment, shall be by Jury; and such Trial shall be held in the State where the said Crimes shall have been committed; but when not committed within any State, the Trial shall be at such Place or Places as the Congress may by Law have directed.

Section. 3. Treason against the United States, shall consist only in levying War against them, or in adhering to their Enemies, giving them Aid and Comfort. No Person shall be convicted of Treason unless on the Testimony of two Witnesses to the same overt Act, or on Confession in open Court.

The Congress shall have Power to declare the Punishment of Treason, but no Attainder of Treason shall work Corruption of Blood, or Forfeiture except during the Life of the Person attainted.

Article. IV.

Section. 1. Full Faith and Credit shall be given in each State to the public Acts, Records, and judical Proceedings of every other State. And the Congress may by general Laws prescribe the Manner in which such Acts, Records and Proceedings shall be proved, and the Effect thereof.

Section. 2. The Citizens of each State shall be entitled to all Privileges and Immunities of Citizens in the several States.

A Person charged in any State with Treason, Felony, or other Crime, who shall flee from Justice, and be found in another State, shall on Demand of the executive Authority of the State from which he fled, be delivered up, to be removed to the State having Jurisdiction of the Crime:

No Person held to Service or Labour in one State, under the Laws thereof, escaping into another, shall, in Consequence of any Law or Regulation therein, be discharged from such Service or Labour, but shall be delivered up on Claim of the Party to whom such Service or Labour may be due.

Section. 3. New States may be admitted by the Congress into this Union; but no new State shall be formed or erected within the Jurisdiction of any other State; nor any State be formed by the

Junction of two or more States, or Parts of States, without the Consent of the Legislatures of the States concerned as well as of the Congress.

The Congress shall have Power to dispose of and make all needful Rules and Regulations respecting the Territory or other Property belonging to the United States; and nothing in this Constitution shall be so construed as to Prejudice any Claims of the United States, or of any particular State.

Section. 4. The United States shall guarantee to every State in this Union a Republican Form of Government, and shall protect each of them against Invasion; and on Application of the Legislature, or of the Executive (when the Legislature cannot be convened) against domestic Violence.

Article. V.

The Congress, whenever two thirds of both Houses shall deem it necessary, shall propose Amendments to this Constitution, or, on the Application of the Legislatures of two thirds of the several States, shall call a Convention for proposing Amendments, which, in either Case, shall be valid to all Intents and Purposes, as Part of this Constitution, when ratified by the Legislatures of three fourths of the several States, or by Conventions in three fourths thereof, as the one or the other Mode of Ratification may be proposed by the Congress; Provided that no Amendment which may be made prior to the Year One thousand eight hundred and eight shall in any Manner affect the first and fourth Clauses in the Ninth Section of the first Article; and that no State, without its Consent, shall be deprived of it's equal Suffrage in the Senate.

Article. VI.

All Debts contracted and Engagements entered into, before the Adoption of this Constitution, shall be as valid against the United States under this Constitution, as under the Confederation.

This Constitution, and the Laws of the United States which shall be made in Pursuance thereof; and all Treaties made, or which shall be made, under the Authority of the United States, shall be the supreme Law of the Land; and the Judges in every

State shall be bound thereby, any Thing in the Constitution or Laws of any State to the Contrary notwithstanding.

The Senators and Representatives before mentioned, and the Members of the several State Legislatures, and all executive and judicial Officers, both of the United States and of the several States, shall be bound by Oath or Affirmation, to support this Constitution; but no religious Test shall ever be required as a Qualification to any Office or public Trust under the United States.

Article. VII.

The Ratification of the Conventions of nine States, shall be sufficient for the Establishment of this Constitution between the States so ratifying the Same.

The Word, "the," being interlined between the seventh and eighth Lines of the first Page, The Word "Thirty" being partly written on an Erazure in the fifteenth Line of the first Page, The Words "is tried" being interlined between the thirty second and thirty third Lines of the first Page and the Word "the" being interlined between the forty third and forty fourth Lines of the second Page.

done in Convention by the Unanimous Consent of the States present the Seventeenth Day of September in the Year of our Lord one thousand seven hundred and Eighty seven and of the Independance of the United States of America the Twelfth In witness whereof We have hereunto subscribed our Names,

G? WASHINGTON—Presid!
    and deputy from Virginia

Attest WILLIAM JACKSON Secretary

New Hampshire	{ John Langdon Nicholas Gilman }
Massachusetts	{ Nathaniel Gorham Rufus King
Connecticut	{ Wm Saml Johnson Roger Sherman
New York	Alexander Hamilton
New Jersey	{ Wil: Livingston David Brearley. Wm Paterson. Jona: Dayton
Pensylvania	{ B Franklin Thomas Mifflin Robt Morris Geo. Clymer Thos FitzSimons Jared Ingersoll James Wilson Gouv Morris
Delaware	{ Geo: Read Gunning Bedford jun John Dickinson Richard Bassett Jaco: Broom
Maryland	{ James McHenry Dan of St Thos Jenifer Danl Carroll
Virginia	{ John Blair— James Madison Jr.
North Carolina	{ Wm Blount Richd Dobbs Spaight. Hu Williamson
South Carolina	{ J. Rutledge Charles Cotesworth Pinckney Charles Pinckney Pierce Butler.
Georgia	{ William Few Abr Baldwin

THE FIRST TEN AMENDMENTS TO THE CONSTITUTION

ARTICLE I

Congress shall make no law respecting an establishment of religion, or prohibiting the free exercise thereof; or abridging the freedom of speech, or of the press; or the right of the people peaceably to assemble, and to petition the Government for a redress of grievances.

ARTICLE II

A well regulated Militia, being necessary to the security of a free State, the right of the people to keep and bear Arms, shall not be infringed.

ARTICLE III

No Soldier shall, in time of peace be quartered in any house, without the consent of the Owner, nor in time of war, but in a manner to be prescribed by law.

ARTICLE IV

The right of the people to be secure in their persons, houses, papers, and effects, against unreasonable searches and seizures, shall not be violated, and no Warrants shall issue, but upon probable cause, supported by Oath or affirmation, and particularly describing the place to be searched, and the persons or things to be seized.

ARTICLE V

No person shall be held to answer for a capital, or otherwise infamous crime, unless on a presentment or indictment of a Grand Jury, except in cases arising in the land or naval forces, or in the Militia, when in actual service in time of War or public danger; nor shall any person be subject for the same offence to be twice put in jeopardy of life or limb; nor shall be compelled in any criminal case to be a witness against himself, nor be deprived of life, liberty, or property, without due process of law; nor shall private property be taken for public use, without just compensation.

Article VI

In all criminal prosecutions, the accused shall enjoy the right to a speedy and public trial, by an impartial jury of the State and district wherein the crime shall have been committed, which district shall have been previously ascertained by law, and to be informed of the nature and cause of the accusation; to be confronted with the witnesses against him; to have compulsory process for obtaining witnesses in his favor, and to have the Assistance of Counsel for his defence.

Article VII

In Suits at common law, where the value in controversy shall exceed twenty dollars, the right of trial by jury shall be preserved, and no fact tried by a jury, shall be otherwise re-examined in any Court of the United States, than according to the rules of the common law.

Article VIII

Excessive bail shall not be required, nor excessive fines imposed, nor cruel and unusual punishments inflicted.

Article IX

The enumeration in the Constitution, of certain rights, shall not be construed to deny or disparage others retained by the people.

Article X

The powers not delegated to the United States by the Constitution, nor prohibited by it to the States, are reserved to the States respectively, or to the people.

SUBSEQUENT AMENDMENTS TO THE CONSTITUTION

Article XI [1]

The Judicial power of the United States shall not be construed to extend to any suit in law or equity, commenced or prosecuted against one of the United States by Citizens of another State, or by Citizens or Subjects of any Foreign State.

Article XII [2]

The Electors shall meet in their respective states, and vote by ballot for President and Vice-President, one of whom, at least, shall not be an inhabitant of the same state with themselves; they shall name in their ballots the person voted for as President, and in distinct ballots the person voted for as Vice-President, and they shall make distinct lists of all persons voted for as President, and of all persons voted for as Vice-President, and of the number of votes for each, which lists they shall sign and certify, and transmit sealed to the seat of the government of the United States, directed to the President of the Senate;—The President of the Senate shall, in the presence of the Senate and House of Representatives, open all the certificates and the votes shall then be counted;—The person having the greatest number of votes for President, shall be the President, if such number be a majority of the whole number of Electors appointed; and if no person have such majority, then from the persons having the highest numbers not exceeding three on the list of those voted for as President, the House of Representatives shall choose immediately, by ballot, the President. But in choosing the President, the votes shall be taken by states, the representation from each state having one vote; a quorum for this purpose shall consist of a member or members from two-thirds

---

[1] The eleventh amendment was declared in a message from the President to Congress, dated the 8th of January, 1798, to have been ratified by the legislatures of three-fourths of the States.

[2] The twelfth amendment, in lieu of the original third paragraph of the first section of the second article, was declared in a proclamation of the Secretary of State, dated the 25th of September, 1804, to have been ratified by the legislatures of three-fourths of the States.

of the states, and a majority of all the states shall be necessary to a choice. And if the House of Representatives shall not choose a President whenever the right of choice shall devolve upon them, before the fourth day of March next following, then the Vice-President shall act as President, as in the case of the death or other constitutional disability of the President. The person having the greatest number of votes as Vice-President, shall be the Vice-President, if such number be a majority of the whole number of Electors appointed, and if no person have a majority, then from the two highest numbers on the list, the Senate shall choose the Vice-President; a quorum for the purpose shall consist of two-thirds of the whole number of Senators, and a majority of the whole number shall be necessary to a choice. But no person constitutionally ineligible to the office of President shall be eligible to that of Vice-President of the United States.

Article XIII [3]

Section 1. Neither slavery nor involuntary servitude except as a punishment for crime whereof the party shall have been duly convicted, shall exist within the United States, or any place subject to their juridsiction.

Section 2. Congress shall have power to enforce this article by appropriate legislation.

Article XIV [4]

Section 1. All persons born or naturalized in the United States, and subject to the jurisdiction thereof, are citizens of the United States and of the State wherein they reside. No State shall make or enforce any law which shall abridge the privileges or immunities of citizens of the United States; nor shall any State deprive any person of life, liberty, or property, without due process of law; nor deny to any person within its jurisdiction the equal protection of the laws.

---

[3] The thirteenth amendment was declared, in a proclamation of the Secretary of State, dated the 18th of December, 1865, to have been ratified by the legislatures of twenty-seven of the thirty-six States.

[4] The fourteenth amendment was, in a proclamation of the Secretary of State, dated the 28th of July, 1868, declared to have been ratified by the legislatures of thirty of the thirty-six States.

SECTION 2. Representatives shall be apportioned among the several States according to their respective numbers, counting the whole number of persons in each State, excluding Indians not taxed. But when the right to vote at any election for the choice of electors for President and Vice President of the United States, Representatives in Congress, the Executive and Judicial officers of a State, or the members of the Legislature thereof, is denied to any of the male inhabitants of such State, being twenty-one years of age, and citizens of the United States, or in any way abridged, except for participation in rebellion, or other crime, the basis of representation therein shall be reduced in the proportion which the number of such male citizens shall bear to the whole number of male citizens twenty-one years of age in such State.

SECTION 3. No person shall be a Senator or Representative in Congress, or elector of President and Vice President, or hold any office, civil or military, under the United States, or under any State, who, having previously taken an oath, as a member of Congress, or as an officer of the United States, or as a member of any State legislature, or as an executive or judicial officer of any State, to support the Constitution of the United States, shall have engaged in insurrection or rebellion against the same, or given aid or comfort to the enemies thereof. But Congress may by a vote of two-thirds of each House, remove such disability.

SECTION 4. The validity of the public debt of the United States, authorized by law, including debts incurred for payment of pensions and bounties for services in suppressing insurrection or rebellion, shall not be questioned. But neither the United States nor any State shall assume or pay any debt or obligation incurred in aid of insurrection or rebellion against the United States, or any claim for the loss or emancipation of any slave; but all such debts, obligations and claims shall be held illegal and void.

SECTION 5. The Congress shall have power to enforce, by appropriate legislation, the provisions of this article.

Formation of the United States

Article XV[5]

Section 1. The right of citizens of the United States to vote shall not be denied or abridged by the United States or by any State on account of race, color, or previous condition of servitude.

Section 2. The Congress shall have power to enforce this article by appropriate legislation.

Article XVI[6]

The Congress shall have power to lay and collect taxes on incomes, from whatever source derived, without apportionment among the several States, and without regard to any census or enumeration.

Article XVII[7]

(1) The Senate of the United States shall be composed of two Senators from each State, elected by the people thereof, for six years; and each Senator shall have one vote. The electors in each State shall have the qualifications requisite for electors of the most numerous branch of the State legislatures.

(2) When vacancies happen in the representation of any State in the Senate, the executive authority of such State shall issue writs of election to fill such vacancies: *Provided*, That the legislature of any State may empower the executive thereof to make temporary appointments until the people fill the vacancies by election as the legislature may direct.

(3) This amendment shall not be so construed as to affect the election or term of any Senator chosen before it becomes valid as part of the Constitution.

Article XVIII[8]

Section 1. After one year from the ratification of this article the manufacture, sale, or transportation of intoxicating liquors

---

[5] The fifteenth amendment was declared, in a proclamation of the Secretay of State, dated March 30, 1870, to have been ratified by the legislatures of twenty-nine of the thirty-seven States.

[6] The sixteenth amendment was declared in an announcement by the Secretary of State, dated February 25, 1913, to have been ratified by the legislatures of thirty-eight of the forty-eight States.

[7] The seventeenth amendment was declared, in an announcement by the Secretary of State, dated May 31, 1913, to have been ratified by the legislatures of thirty-six of the forth-eight States

[8] The eighteenth amendment was declared, in an announcement by the Acting Secretary of State, dated January 29, 1919, to have been ratified by the legislatures of thirty-six of the forty-eight States.

within, the importation thereof into, or the exportation thereof from the United States and all territory subject to the jurisdiction thereof for beverage purposes is hereby prohibited.

SECTION 2. The Congress and the several States shall have concurrent power to enforce this article by appropriate legislation.

SECTION 3. This article shall be inoperative unless it shall have been ratified as an amendment to the Constitution by the legislatures of the several States, as provided in the Constitution, within seven years from the date of the submission hereof to the States by the Congress.

ARTICLE XIX

The right of the citizens of the United States to vote shall not be denied or abridged by the United States or by any State on account of sex.

Congress shall have power to enforce this article by appropriate legislation.[*]

---

[*] The nineteenth amendment was declared, in an announcement of the Secretary of State, dated August 26, 1920, to have been ratified by the legislatures of thirty-eight of the forty-eight States.

AMENDMENT XX
(Ratified January 23, 1933)

Section 1. The terms of the President and Vice President shall end at noon on the 20th day of January, and the terms of Senators and Representatives, at noon on the 3rd day of January, of the years in which such terms would have ended if this article has not been ratified; and the terms of their successors shall then begin.

Section 2. The Congress shall assemble at least once in every year, and such meeting shall begin at noon on the 3rd day of January, unless they shall by law appoint a different day.

Section 3. If, at the time fixed for the beginning of the term of the President, the President elect shall have died, the Vice President elect shall become President. If a President shall not have been chosen before the time fixed for the beginning of his term, or if the President elect shall have failed to qualify, then the Vice President elect shall act as President until a President shall have qualified; and the Congress may by law provide for the case wherein neither a President elect nor a Vice President elect shall have qualified, declaring who shall then act as President, or the manner in which one who is to act shall be selected, and such person shall act accordingly until a President or Vice President shall have qualified.

Section 4. The Congress may by law provide for the case of the death of any of the persons from whom the House of Representatives may choose a President whenever the right of choice shall have devolved upon them, and for the case of the death of any of the persons from whom the Senate may choose a Vice President whenever the right of choice shall have devolved upon them.

Section 5. Sections 1 and 2 shall take effect on the 15th day of October following the ratification of this article.

Section 6. This article shall be inoperative unless it shall have been ratified as an amendment to the Constitution by the legislatures of three-fourths of the several States within seven years from the date of its submission.

AMENDMENT XXI
(Ratified December 5, 1933)

Section 1. The eighteenth article of amendment to the Constitution of the United States is hereby repealed.

Section 2. The transportation or importation into any State, Territory, or possession of the United States for delivery or use therein of intoxicating liquors, in violation of the laws thereof, is hereby prohibited.

Section 3. This article shall be inoperative unless it shall have been ratified as an amendment to the Constitution by conventions in the several States, as provided in the Constitution, within seven years from the date of the submission hereof to the States by the Congress.

AMENDMENT XXII
(Ratified February 27, 1951)

Section 1. No person shall be elected to the office of the President more than twice, and no person who has held the office of President, or acted as President, for more that two years of a term to which some other person was elected President shall be elected to the office of the President more than once. But this article shall not apply to any person holding the office of President when this Article was proposed by the Congress, and shall not prevent any person who may be holding the office of President, of acting as President, during the term within which this Article becomes operative from holding the office of President or acting as President during the remainder of such term.

Section 2. This article shall be inoperative unless it shall have been ratified as an amendment to the Constitution by the legislatures of the three-fourths of the several States within seven years from the date of its submission to the States by the Congress.

AMENDMENT XXIII
(Ratified March 29, 1961)

Section 1. The District constituting the seat of Government of the United States shall appoint in such manner as the Congress may direct:

A number of electors of President and Vice President equal to the whole number of Senators and Representatives in Congress to which the District would be entitled if it were a State, but in no event more than the least populous State; they shall be in addition to those appointed by the State, but they shall be considered, for the purposes of the election of President and Vice President, to be electors appointed by a State; and they shall meet in the District and perform such duties as provided by the twelfth article of amendment.

Section 2. The Congress shall have power to enforce this article by appropriate legislation.

AMENDMENT XXIV
(Ratified January 23, 1964)

Section 1. The right of citizens of the United States to vote in any primary or other election for President or Vice President, for electors for President or Vice President, or for Senator or Representative in Congress, shall not be denied or abridged by the United States or any State by reason of failure to pay any poll tax or other tax.

Section 2. The Congress shall have the power to enforce this article by appropriate legislation.

AMENDMENT XXV
(Ratified February 10, 1967)

Section 1. In the case the removal of the President from office or of his death or resignation, the Vice President shall become president.

Section 2. Whenever there is a vacancy in the office of the Vice President, the President shall nominate a Vice President who shall take office upon the confirmation by a majority vote of both Houses of Congress.

Section 3. Whenever the President transmits to the President pro tempore of the Senate and the Speaker of the House of Representatives his written declaration that he is unable to discharge the powers and duties of his office, and until he transmits to them a written declaration to the contrary, such powers and duties shall be discharged by the Vice President as Acting President.

Section 4. Whenever the Vice President and a majority of either the principal officers of the executive departments or of such other body as Congress may by law provide, transmit to the President Pro Tempore of the Senate and the Speaker of the House of Representatives their written declaration that the President is unable to discharge the powers and duties of his office, the Vice President shall immediately assume the powers and duties of the office as Acting President.

Thereafter, when the President transmits to the President Pro Tempore of the Senate and the Speaker of the House of Representatives his written declaration that no inability exists, he shall resume the powers and duties of his office unless the Vice President and a majority of either the principal officers of the executive department or of such other body as Congress may by law provide, transmit within four days to the President Pro Tempore of the Senate and the Speaker of the House of Representatives their written declaration that the President is unable to discharge the powers and duties of his office. Thereupon Congress shall decide the issue, assembling within forty-eight hours for that purpose if not in session. If the Congress, within twenty-one days after receipt of the latter written declaration, or, if Congress is not in session, within twenty-one days after Congress is required to assemble, determines by two-thirds vote of both Houses that the President is unable to discharge the powers and duties of his office, the Vice President shall continue to discharge the same as Acting President; otherwise, the President shall resume the powers and duties of his office.

AMENDMENT XXVI
(Ratified July 1, 1971)

Section 1. The right of citizens of the United States, who are eighteen years of age or older, to vote shall not be denied or abridged by the United States or by any State on account of age.

Section 2. The Congress shall have the power to enforce this article by appropriate legislation.

RESOLUTIONS OF 1798
In the House of Delegates
Friday, December 2, 1798

[1] *Resolved*, That the General Assembly of Virginia doth unequivocally express a firm resolution to maintain and defend the Constitution of the United States, and the Constitution of this State, against every aggression either foreign or domestic; and that they will support the Government of the United States in all measures warranted by the former.

[2] That this Assembly most solemnly declares a warm attachment to the union of the States, to maintain which it pledges all its powers; and that, for this end, it is their duty to watch over and oppose every infraction of those principles which constitute the only basis of that Union, because a faithful observance of them can alone secure its existence and the public happiness.

[3] That this Assembly doth explicitly and peremptorily declare that it views the powers of the Federal Government as resulting from the compact to which the States are parties, as limited by the plain sense and intention of the instrument constituting that compact; as no further valid than they are authorized by the grants enumerated in that compact; and that in case of a deliberate, palpable, and dangerous exercise of other powers not granted by the said compact, the States, who are parties thereto, have the right and are in duty bound to interpose for arresting the progress of the evil, and for maintaining within their respective limits the authorities, rights, and liberties appertaining to them.

[4] That the General Assembly doth also express its deep regret, that a spirit has in sundry instances been manifested by the Federal Government to enlarge its powers by forced constructions of the constitutional charter which defines them; and that indications have appeared of a design to expound certain general phrases (which, having been copied from the very limited grant of powers in the former Articles of Confederation, were the less liable to be misconstrued) so as to consolidate the States, by degrees, into one sovereignty, the obvious tendency and inevitable result of which would be to transform the present republican system of the United States into an absolute, or, at best, a mixed monarchy.

[5] That the General Assembly doth particularly protest against the palpable and alarming infractions of the Constitution in the two late cases of the "Alien and Sedition Acts," passed at the last session of Congress; the first of which exercises a power nowhere delegated to the Federal Government and which, by uniting legislative and judicial powers to those of [the] executive, subvert the general principles of free government, as well as the particular organization and positive provisions of the Federal Constitution; and the other of which acts exercises, in like manner, a power not delegated by the Constitution, but, on the contrary, expressly and positively forbidden by one of the amendments thereto,--a power which more than any other, ought to produce universal alarm, because it is levelled against the right of freely examining public characters and measures, and of free communication among the people thereon, which has ever been justly deemed the only effectual guardian of every other right.

[6] That this State having by its Convention which ratified the Federal Constitution expressly declared that, among other essential rights, "the liberty of conscience and of the press cannot be cancelled, abridged, restrained or modified by any authority of the United States," and from its extreme anxiety to guard these rights from every possible attack of sophistry and ambition, having, with other States, recommended an amendment for that purpose, which amendment was in due time annexed to the Constitution,--it would mark a reproachful inconsistency and criminal degeneracy, if an indifference were now shown to the palpable violation of one of the rights thus declared and secured, and to the establishment of a precedent which may be fatal to the other.

[7] That the good people of this Commonwealth, having ever felt and continuing to feel the most sincere affection for their brethren of the other States, the truest anxiety for establishing and perpetuating the union of all and the most scrupulous fidelity to that Constitution, which is the pledge of mutual friendship, and the instrument of mutual happiness, the General Assembly doth solemnly appeal to the like dispositions of the other States, in confidence that they will concur with this Commonwealth in declaring, as it does hereby declare, that the acts aforesaid are unconstitutional; and that the necessary and proper measures will be taken by each for co-operating with this State, in maintaining unimpaired authorities, rights, and liberties reserved to the States respectively, or to the people.

[8] That the Governor be desired to transmit a copy of the foregoing resolutions to the Executive authority of each of the other States, with a request that the same be communicated to the Legislature thereof; and that a copy be furnished to each of the Senators and Representatives representing this State in the Congress of the United States.

RESOLUTIONS OF 1799,
In the House of Delegates
Friday, January 4, 1799

Resolved, That the General Assembly of Virginia will cooperate with the authorities of the United States in maintaining the independence, Union and Constitution thereof, against the hostilities or intrigues of all foreign Powers whatsoever; and that although differences of opinion do exist in relation to internal and domestic measures, yet a charge that there is a party in this Commonwealth under the influence of any foreign Power is unfounded and calumnious.

Resolved, That the General Assembly do, and will always, behold with indignation, depredations on our commerce, insults on our citizens, impressments of our seamen, or any other injuries committed on the people or Government of the United States by foreign nations.

Resolved, Nevertheless, that our security from invasion and the force of our militia render a standing army unnecessary; that the policy of the United States forbids a war of aggression; that our whole reliance ought to be on ourselves; and therefore, that while we will repel invasion at every hazard, we shall deplore and deprecate the evils of war for any other cause.

Resolved, That a copy of the foregoing resolution be sent to each of the Senators and Representatives of this State in Congress.

NO STRINGS ATTACHED?

Have you ever noticed the wonderment in the eyes of a child, captivated by the artful manipulations of a master puppeteer? The child is mystified by the illusion that the puppet is nothing less than a living, breathing creature. But from the moment that the child is either shown or perceives the strings, the fantasy world of puppets is forever vanquished. This perceptual change will make futile all future attempts to convince him that puppets are just *little people*. From that moment the child's eyes can always see and follow the strings to the hands of the puppeteer.

In the real world, there are living, breathing creatures called men. These creatures like to project the impression that they are the "captains of their own souls and the masters of their fate." When in reality, they are more often *controlled* than controlling. But, instead of looking for their own strings, most men maintain a naiveté that surpasses that of the most gullible child. In psychology this might be called a "defense mechanism." Their response to certain kinds of, *fully documented*, bad news is "Oh, I don't subscribe to all those wild-eyed conspiracy theories!" Are we to believe, that in the real world, evil men do not meet to make evil plans and then try to bring their schemes into reality? I think I can never be *that* naive again, since I am beginning to perceive the heavy cords of **BANKING, MONETARY CONTROL, TAXATION, DOMINATION** and even **MEGALOMANIA**. There *have* been real people named Marx, Hitler, Lenin, Stalin and Mao. The history of what they accomplished, and of what they were attempting, is solid evidence that there is something in man, perhaps his worst flaw, that can cause him to seek the total domination of his fellow man. And yet, this must be only the "tip of the iceberg" for if none of these had had financial, moral, or *psycho-political* support, they might have enjoyed the anonymity they so richly deserved. But they all met secretly with others to plan and *fund* their nefarious schemes. Are we to believe that all the lessons of history can be discarded and we will soon be ushered into a utopian age by the collective *virtue* of humankind? Is this a child's dream or a "fool's paradise?" Did Hitler's tanks roll into France without fuel? No, *someone* supplied the fuel and all the usual resources required to prosecute war. Someone or some group who controlled those resources saw a personal or collective advantage in the possible success of a Hitler. Can you imagine the magnitude of resources that might be brought to bear if someone were planning nothing less than the total domination of the whole world?

The Constitution of The United States stands as one of the final and most formidable obstacles to **One World Government**. Its enemies have been working night and day almost since its birth to destroy this uniquely **American Document**. If we fail to restore its authority and pass it on to our posterity, it is doubtless that barring **Divine Intervention**, they will certainly **Live** and **Die as Slaves!** Is it once again time to choose between the "**Bowl of Pottage**" and the **Sacred Birthright**?

ONCE YOU CAN FOLLOW THE STRINGS, THEY WILL NEVER DISAPPEAR AGAIN! SOONER OR LATER THEY MUST LEAD TO THE HANDS OF THE MASTER PUPPETEER!

A life not committed to the endless quest for **TRUTH** is ultimately bound to embrace **SLAVERY** as if it were **SALVATION!**